Dedication

This book is dedicated to all who cherish their friendships, explore the joy of discovering new things. May you always find a Luna or a Max in your life—someone to laugh with, grow with, and conquer the big world hand in hand.

The Adventure of True Friendship in the Big City

Community and Society

Eleanor Sutton

Published by The Good Child Bookstore, 2024.

While every precaution has been taken in the preparation of this book, the publisher assumes no responsibility for errors or omissions, or for damages resulting from the use of the information contained herein.

THE ADVENTURE OF TRUE FRIENDSHIP IN THE BIG CITY

First edition. September 30, 2024.

Copyright © 2024 Eleanor Sutton.

ISBN: 979-8227166234

Written by Eleanor Sutton.

Also by Eleanor Sutton

Community and Society
The Adventure of True Friendship in the Big City

Virtue Series
How the Kindness Seed Grew Into a Giant Tree

Table of Contents

Preface 1
Chapter 1: The Meeting on Main Street 2
Chapter 2: The Subway Adventure 6
Chapter 3: A Rooftop Picnic 9
Chapter 4: The Pigeon Patrol 13
Chapter 5: The Mystery of the Missing Acorns 17
Chapter 6: The Thunderstorm 20
Chapter 7: The Great City Race 24
Chapter 8: The Midnight Adventure 27
Chapter 9: The Old Library 30
Chapter 10: The Art of Flying 33
Chapter 11: The Friendship Festival 37
Chapter 12: The Hidden Tunnel 40
Chapter 13: The Concert in Central Park 44
Chapter 14: The Mischievous Monkey 47
Chapter 15: The City Marathon 50
Chapter 16: The Winter's Tale 54
Chapter 17: The Mysterious Owl 58
Chapter 18: The Night of the Lanterns 63
Chapter 19: The Lost Puppy 68
Chapter 20: The Day the Sky Turned Red 72
Chapter 21: The Heart of the City 76
Chapter 22: The Goodbye That Wasn't 79
Chapter 23: The Grand Reunion 83
Chapter 24: The Whispering Wind 89
Chapter 25: The Festival of Friends 93

Preface

Friendship is one of life's greatest gifts, and for children, it plays a vital role in shaping how they see the world and navigate its many ups and downs. In *The Adventure of True Friendship in the Big City*, I wanted to capture the essence of that special bond. Max and Luna, despite their differences, find strength in each other as they face challenges and grow closer with each adventure. Through their journey, this story highlights important lessons about kindness, resilience, and trust. My hope is that young readers will see themselves in Max and Luna and be inspired to embrace the power of true friendship.

Chapter 1: The Meeting on Main Street

Max the squirrel lived a simple, quiet life. His days were spent scampering through the park, gathering acorns and watching the world go by from the comfort of a tall oak tree. He liked the quiet, the rustle of the leaves, and the way the park provided a peaceful escape from the bustling big city just beyond its borders. Max kept to himself and rarely ventured out of his small world. The city, with its loud noises and constant movement, was a place he didn't understand and, quite frankly, had no desire to explore.

But one crisp autumn morning, as Max searched for acorns near the edge of the park, something caught his attention. The sound of the city seemed louder than usual. Curiosity, a feeling Max rarely indulged, got the better of him, and he found himself drawn closer to the towering buildings of Main Street. The acorns were scarce in the park that day, and he figured he might find more if he ventured just a little farther.

Before he knew it, Max had crossed into the city, and the peaceful trees were behind him. The ground beneath his paws turned to pavement, and the trees gave way to towering buildings made of concrete and glass. Max, suddenly aware of how far he had wandered, began to panic. The city was overwhelming, filled with strange sounds, fast-moving cars, and people rushing by without even noticing the small, nervous squirrel.

Max darted from corner to corner, looking for a way back, but everything seemed unfamiliar. The loud honking of cars made him flinch, and the crowds of people made him feel smaller than ever. His heart pounded in his chest, and he felt completely lost.

From high above, Luna, a pigeon who had lived in the city her entire life, was perched on a streetlight, watching the scene below. Luna loved the hustle and bustle of the city. She knew every nook and cranny, every shortcut and hidden corner. As she surveyed the busy street, she spotted the panicked squirrel darting back and forth. She tilted her head, curious. It wasn't every day that she saw a squirrel so far from the park.

Deciding to investigate, Luna swooped down and landed gracefully in front of Max, who immediately froze, unsure of what to expect from this city bird. Luna looked at him with a curious glint in her eye. "Are you lost?" she asked in a voice that was calm and confident.

Max, still cautious, nodded slowly. "I... I don't belong here," he stammered. "I'm from the park. I just came to find some acorns, and now I can't find my way back."

Luna smiled. "Well, you're in luck. I know this city like the back of my wing. I can help you get back to the park."

Max hesitated. He had always been wary of pigeons. In the park, the squirrels mostly kept to themselves, and the pigeons were known to be a bit too bold for Max's liking. But right now, he was lost, and Luna seemed like his only hope of getting home. "I guess... I guess I could use some help," Max said, trying to hide his reluctance.

Without waiting for a formal agreement, Luna flapped her wings and took off into the air, hovering just above Max. "Follow me!" she called out as she soared down the street.

Max hurried after her, dodging pedestrians and scurrying across busy intersections as Luna guided him through the maze of streets. The city, though still overwhelming, seemed a little less frightening with Luna leading the way. She moved with ease, expertly navigating the chaos that had earlier terrified Max.

As they made their way back to the park, Luna chatted non-stop about the city. "You know, the city isn't as bad as it looks," she said. "There's always something new to see, something exciting happening. You just have to know where to look."

Max, still catching his breath from dodging a particularly large crowd of humans, wasn't sure he agreed. "I like the quiet of the park," he said. "It's peaceful there. This..." he gestured to the bustling streets, "this is too much for me."

Luna landed on a bench just outside the park's entrance and looked at Max thoughtfully. "I get that. The park is nice, but there's a lot you're missing out on by staying in one place. The city can be noisy and busy, sure, but it's also full of opportunities, new experiences, and friends you haven't met yet."

Max wasn't sure how to respond. He had never thought about the city like that before. To him, it had always been a place to avoid, a world of chaos and noise that he wanted no part of. But Luna made it sound... interesting.

As they entered the park, Max felt a wave of relief wash over him. The familiar trees, the cool shade, and the gentle rustling of leaves welcomed him back. He turned to Luna, who was perched on a low branch, watching him with a friendly smile.

"Thanks," Max said, feeling grateful but still a bit unsure. "I don't think I would've made it back without your help."

Luna winked. "Anytime, Max. And if you ever feel like exploring the city again, you know where to find me."

Max nodded, still not entirely convinced that the city was a place he wanted to explore. But something about Luna's confidence and enthusiasm made him wonder if maybe, just maybe, there was more to the city than he had given it credit for.

As Luna flew off into the sky, Max found himself thinking about their brief adventure. It had been scary at times, but it had also been kind of exciting. And Luna, though so different from him, had been a good friend—brave, confident, and helpful when he needed her most.

Max climbed up his tree and settled into his cozy nook, surrounded by the quiet he loved so much. But for the first time, the quiet didn't feel quite the same. He couldn't stop thinking about the city, and about Luna.

Lessons Learned

THE ADVENTURE OF TRUE FRIENDSHIP IN THE BIG CITY 5

1. Sometimes stepping out of your comfort zone leads to unexpected friendships.
2. It's okay to ask for help when you're lost.
3. Differences between friends can make a relationship more interesting and valuable.
4. The unknown can be scary, but having a friend by your side makes it easier.
5. First impressions aren't always accurate; getting to know someone can change your perspective.
6. Exploring new places can open your eyes to experiences you never imagined.
7. True friends offer help without expecting anything in return.

Chapter 2: The Subway Adventure

The sun was just beginning to set over the city skyline when Max found himself in a situation he never imagined. After his adventure with Luna the day before, Max had cautiously returned to the edge of the park, still hesitant about venturing too far into the city again. But as fate would have it, he found himself caught up in the busiest, loudest, and most chaotic part of the city: the subway.

It all started when Max, trying to gather more acorns to prepare for the coming winter, wandered a little too close to the subway entrance. He had heard about the subway from other animals in the park—stories of underground tunnels where giant machines roared through the dark, ferrying humans from place to place. Max had always been terrified of the idea. The noise, the crowds, and the confined spaces all sounded too much for his liking. But as he stood near the entrance, curiosity got the better of him once again.

Before he knew it, Max had crept closer to the subway stairs. Just a peek, he told himself. He would just take a quick look and then return to the park. But as he edged forward, something unexpected happened. A sudden gust of wind from the tunnel blew his pile of carefully gathered acorns out of his paws. Max scrambled to catch them, but they tumbled down the subway stairs and into the darkness below.

Max stood frozen at the top of the stairs, torn between his fear of the subway and his need to retrieve the acorns. He took a deep breath, telling himself that he would just go down for a moment, grab the acorns, and get out as fast as he could. He gingerly stepped onto the first stair, then the second, and before he knew it, he was halfway down the staircase, the noise of the city above fading into the background.

The air grew colder as he descended, and the sounds of the subway grew louder. Max's heart pounded in his chest as he reached the bottom of the stairs and found himself standing on the platform. The ground rumbled beneath his feet as a train roared past, causing him to leap back in fright. This was definitely not like the quiet park he was used to.

Max spotted his acorns scattered across the platform and quickly began gathering them, trying to calm his racing heart. But just as he collected the last one, he heard a strange sound—a loud whoosh of air, followed by the distant rumbling of another approaching train. Max's fur stood on end as the sound grew louder and louder. He realized, too late, that he was standing too close to the edge of the platform.

Before he could react, a crowd of humans surged forward, pushing and shoving to board the oncoming train. In the chaos, Max was swept up in the wave of people and accidentally stumbled into the subway car just as the doors slid shut behind him.

Panic surged through Max as the train lurched forward, speeding into the dark tunnel. The walls of the subway car were closing in on him, and the noise was deafening. Max darted around the car, looking for a way out, but there was no escape. He was trapped underground, hurtling through the city at lightning speed.

Just as Max was about to completely lose his nerve, a familiar voice called out above the din. "Max! What are you doing here?"

Max looked up and saw Luna perched on a handlebar, her eyes wide with surprise. "Luna?" Max gasped. "I... I didn't mean to get on the subway! I was just trying to get my acorns, and then... everything happened so fast!"

Luna fluttered down to his side and placed a comforting wing on his shoulder. "Don't worry, Max. I'll help you get out of here. You're lucky I was on this train—I was heading uptown for my evening flight practice."

Max felt a wave of relief wash over him. He wasn't alone. Luna was here, and she seemed completely at ease in the subway, as if she had been riding the trains her whole life. "How do you do it, Luna?"

Max asked, his voice trembling. "How do you handle all this noise and chaos?"

Luna smiled. "It's all about knowing the rhythm of the city. Once you get used to it, the subway can be a great way to get around. It's fast, and there's always something interesting happening."

Max wasn't sure if he would ever get used to it. But for now, all he wanted was to get back to the park, where things were quiet and predictable. "Can we get off at the next stop?" he asked, trying to keep the panic out of his voice.

"Of course," Luna said, nodding reassuringly. "Just follow me, and I'll show you how to navigate the subway like a pro."

When the train screeched to a halt at the next station, Luna led Max out of the car and up the stairs to the street above. Max breathed a sigh of relief as they emerged into the open air, the noise of the subway fading into the background. He had made it out, thanks to Luna.

Lessons Learned

1. Facing your fears, even when they seem overwhelming, can lead to growth.
2. Having a friend by your side makes challenges easier to overcome.
3. The city, though chaotic, has its own rhythm that can be understood with time.
4. It's okay to feel scared, but it's important to trust in your abilities and push forward.
5. Sometimes, the scariest moments can teach you the most about yourself.
6. Friends can introduce you to new experiences that you might otherwise avoid.
7. There's always a way out of a difficult situation if you stay calm and trust those around you.

Chapter 3: A Rooftop Picnic

Luna had been talking about the rooftop garden for weeks, ever since she and Max first became friends. She had a way of making everything in the city sound magical, even places that Max would never think to explore. To him, rooftops were just for birds, high up in the air where squirrels like him didn't belong. But to Luna, the city's rooftops were secret worlds, hidden away from the busy streets below.

One warm afternoon, Luna convinced Max to join her for a picnic on one of her favorite rooftops. Max was hesitant, as usual. He liked the comfort of the park, the feel of solid ground beneath his paws. But Luna had been so excited, and Max didn't want to disappoint his friend.

"Come on, Max," Luna said, fluttering around him as he stood at the base of the tall building. "It'll be fun! The view is amazing, and the garden up there is full of delicious treats."

Max looked up at the towering structure, feeling a knot of anxiety form in his stomach. "I don't know, Luna. I'm not really a fan of heights."

Luna landed beside him and nudged him with her wing. "I promise, you'll be safe. And I'll be right there with you the whole time."

Max took a deep breath. He had learned to trust Luna over the past few weeks. She had helped him navigate the city, face his fears, and try new things. If Luna thought the rooftop was worth exploring, maybe it wasn't such a bad idea.

"Okay," Max said, trying to sound more confident than he felt. "Let's go."

Luna grinned and took off into the air, circling above the building. "There's a fire escape around the side. You can climb up from there!"

Max followed her around the corner, finding the rusty metal ladder that led up the side of the building. He hesitated for a moment, his paws gripping the cool metal, but then he reminded himself that Luna was waiting for him at the top. Slowly, he began to climb.

The higher he went, the more his fear started to fade. The view of the city below was breathtaking. Max could see the park in the distance, the tops of trees swaying in the breeze, and the sun setting over the skyline. It was... beautiful. He had never seen the city from this angle before.

By the time Max reached the top, Luna was already perched on a small stone bench in the middle of a lush garden. Flowers of all colors bloomed around her, and vines draped over the edges of the rooftop like curtains. There was a small fountain trickling water, and the scent of fresh herbs filled the air.

"See?" Luna said, spreading her wings as if to show off the view. "Isn't it amazing?"

Max nodded, speechless. He had never imagined a place like this could exist in the city. It was peaceful, almost as quiet as the park, but with the added bonus of the city's energy humming softly in the background.

Luna unpacked a basket filled with treats she had gathered from various parts of the city—seeds from the market, berries from a community garden, and even a few special nuts she had found near the river. Max couldn't help but smile as they spread the food out on a soft blanket, the rooftop garden feeling like their own little secret hideaway.

As they ate, Max realized how much he had changed since meeting Luna. Just a few weeks ago, he would never have considered leaving the safety of the park, let alone climbing to the top of a building for a picnic. But now, sitting with his friend, watching the sun dip below the horizon, he felt a sense of calm and happiness that he hadn't expected.

"You know," Max said between bites, "I didn't think I'd enjoy this, but... I'm glad I came."

THE ADVENTURE OF TRUE FRIENDSHIP IN THE BIG CITY

Luna beamed. "I knew you'd like it! There's so much more to the city than what you see from the ground. You just have to be willing to explore."

Max looked out over the city, the twinkling lights of the buildings reflecting in his eyes. "I guess I've been too focused on staying safe. I never thought about all the things I might be missing."

Luna nodded. "It's okay to like what's familiar, but sometimes stepping outside of that comfort zone can lead to amazing experiences. And it's even better when you have a friend to share it with."

Max smiled, feeling a warmth in his chest. Luna was right. The world was bigger than the park, and with Luna by his side, he felt brave enough to explore it.

As the evening sky turned from orange to deep purple, Max and Luna lay back on the blanket, watching the stars appear one by one. It was quiet now, just the soft rustle of the wind through the garden and the distant hum of the city below.

Max realized that compromise wasn't just about trying new things—it was about understanding that sometimes, stepping into someone else's world could make your own life richer. Luna had shown him a part of the city he never would have seen on his own, and in doing so, she had given him a new appreciation for adventure.

When it was time to leave, Max felt a sense of contentment. He had faced his fear of heights and discovered something beautiful in the process. And though he still loved the park, he knew that there was so much more out there to explore.

"Thanks for bringing me here, Luna," Max said as they made their way back down the fire escape. "I didn't realize how much I needed this."

Luna fluttered beside him, her wings glowing softly in the fading light. "Anytime, Max. That's what friends are for."

Lessons Learned

1. Compromise allows us to experience new things we wouldn't try on our own.
2. Sometimes, stepping outside of your comfort zone can lead to amazing discoveries.
3. Friendship is about sharing experiences and seeing the world from different perspectives.
4. Trusting a friend can help you overcome fears and anxieties.
5. The world is full of hidden beauty, even in places you wouldn't expect.
6. Adventure doesn't always mean danger; it can also mean finding peace in new places.
7. The best experiences are often those shared with someone you care about.

Chapter 4: The Pigeon Patrol

Max had begun to settle into his new friendship with Luna. They spent most afternoons together, exploring the city and learning more about each other. For Max, Luna had become a guide, helping him navigate the big city in ways he never imagined. And for Luna, Max was a grounding presence, reminding her of the peace and stillness that sometimes got lost in the chaos of city life.

One afternoon, as they were walking through the park, Luna started talking about a special group she was part of—the Pigeon Patrol.

"What's the Pigeon Patrol?" Max asked, his curiosity piqued.

Luna puffed out her chest with pride. "We're a group of pigeons who help out around the city. We look out for lost animals, guide them home, and sometimes even help humans who've lost things. It's all about giving back to the community."

Max blinked. "You... help people?"

"Of course!" Luna said with a grin. "Just because we live in a big, busy city doesn't mean we shouldn't look out for each other. The Pigeon Patrol helps make sure everyone stays safe."

Max was impressed. He had never thought of pigeons as helpers, especially in a place as big and complicated as the city. "That sounds... really important," he said slowly. "Do you think I could help?"

Luna looked at Max, her eyes twinkling with excitement. "I was hoping you'd say that! I think you'd be great on the Pigeon Patrol. We could use a clever squirrel like you to help with our missions."

Max felt a little nervous, but also excited. The idea of helping others was something that resonated with him, even though he wasn't sure how he could contribute. But if Luna believed in him, then maybe he could find a way to make a difference.

Later that day, Luna introduced Max to the rest of the Pigeon Patrol. They met in a hidden corner of the park, near a large oak tree where a group of pigeons had gathered. Each pigeon had a sense of purpose, their feathers sleek and their eyes sharp.

"This is Max," Luna said, her voice full of pride. "He's new to the city, but he's already proven himself to be a great friend and a quick learner."

The pigeons all nodded in approval, and Max felt a small surge of confidence. Maybe he could do this after all.

The leader of the group, a wise old pigeon named Greta, stepped forward. "We're glad to have you, Max. Our next mission is to help a lost kitten. It's been wandering around the city, trying to find its way home. We've tracked it to an alley near the bakery, but we need someone small and quick to go in and lead it out. Do you think you can handle that?"

Max swallowed hard. A lost kitten? He had never done anything like this before. But he looked at Luna, who gave him an encouraging nod, and he knew he had to try. "I'll do it," he said, his voice stronger than he felt.

The Pigeon Patrol took flight, with Max following closely on foot. They led him through the busy streets, past towering buildings and bustling markets, until they reached a narrow alleyway near the bakery. The smell of freshly baked bread filled the air, but Max's mind was focused on the task at hand.

"There," Luna whispered, pointing with her wing.

Max peered into the shadows and saw a small, frightened kitten huddled behind a pile of boxes. Its eyes were wide, and its tiny body trembled with fear.

Taking a deep breath, Max approached slowly, trying not to startle the kitten. "Hey there," he said softly. "It's okay. I'm here to help you."

The kitten looked up at him with wide, scared eyes, but didn't move. Max knew he had to gain its trust if he was going to lead it to safety.

THE ADVENTURE OF TRUE FRIENDSHIP IN THE BIG CITY

He crouched down, keeping his movements slow and gentle. "I know you're scared," he continued. "But you don't have to be. I can take you home."

The kitten blinked, still unsure, but it didn't run away. Max reached out a paw, offering a piece of bread he had saved from their picnic earlier. The kitten sniffed the bread cautiously, then took a tentative bite.

"There you go," Max said, his voice soothing. "See? I'm a friend."

After a few more moments, the kitten seemed to relax, and Max carefully led it out of the alley, back toward the street where the Pigeon Patrol was waiting.

"Well done, Max!" Luna called out as they emerged from the shadows.

Greta nodded approvingly. "You've done a great job. This kitten is safe now, thanks to you."

Max felt a surge of pride. He had never thought of himself as a hero, but helping the kitten had shown him that even small acts of kindness could make a big difference.

Max and Luna returned to the park, Max felt a new sense of purpose. The Pigeon Patrol had shown him that even in a big, overwhelming city, there was always room to help those in need. And with Luna by his side, he knew he could face any challenge that came his way.

Lessons Learned

1. Helping others, even in small ways, can make a big difference.
2. Being brave means stepping outside of your comfort zone to do the right thing.
3. Everyone, no matter how small, can contribute to their community.
4. Kindness and patience are key to earning trust, especially in difficult situations.

5. Friends can inspire you to do things you never thought possible.
6. Working as a team can accomplish more than working alone.
7. Even in a big, busy city, there's always a place for compassion and care.

Chapter 5: The Mystery of the Missing Acorns

Max had spent weeks gathering acorns for the winter. He had carefully stored them in his favorite hollow tree, confident that he had enough to last through the cold months ahead. But one morning, when he went to check on his stash, he found the hollow tree empty. His acorns were gone.

At first, Max thought he had made a mistake. Maybe he had put them in a different tree? He scurried around the park, checking all of his usual hiding spots, but every single one was empty. His heart sank. Someone had stolen his acorns.

Max felt a mix of anger and confusion. Who could have done this? The animals in the park were usually friendly, and no one had ever stolen from him before. But now, with winter just around the corner, he had no food left, and he didn't know what to do.

He decided to ask Luna for help. If anyone could solve a mystery in the city, it was Luna.

When Max explained the situation, Luna nodded thoughtfully. "We'll figure this out, Max. Don't worry. We'll track down whoever took your acorns."

Max wasn't sure how they were going to do that, but he trusted Luna. She always had a plan.

They started by searching the park, looking for clues. Max showed Luna where he had stored the acorns, and Luna examined the area carefully. "Hmm," she said, studying the ground. "Look at these footprints."

Max peered down at the ground and saw tiny tracks leading away from the tree. "Those don't look like squirrel tracks," he said slowly.

"They're not," Luna agreed. "They're too small. I think we're dealing with a chipmunk."

Max blinked. A chipmunk? He hadn't even thought about that. Chipmunks were known for being sneaky, but Max didn't know any chipmunks personally.

"Do you think a chipmunk took my acorns?" Max asked, feeling a little disheartened.

"It's possible," Luna said. "But we won't know for sure until we follow these tracks."

Together, Max and Luna followed the tiny footprints through the park and into the city. The tracks led them to a small, quiet alleyway behind a bakery, where they found a pile of scattered acorns.

"That's them!" Max exclaimed, recognizing his stash immediately.

But just as Max was about to collect his acorns, a small figure darted out from behind a trash can. It was a chipmunk, its cheeks stuffed with food, and it looked guilty as soon as it saw Max and Luna.

The chipmunk froze, eyes wide. "I... I didn't mean to steal," it stammered. "I just didn't have enough food for winter, and I saw your stash. I thought you wouldn't miss a few acorns..."

Max felt a surge of sympathy. The chipmunk looked scared and hungry, and Max realized that it hadn't taken the acorns out of malice—it had taken them out of desperation.

Luna stepped forward. "We understand," she said gently. "But stealing isn't the right way to solve your problem. If you had asked, Max would have been happy to share."

The chipmunk hung its head. "I'm sorry. I didn't know what else to do."

Max thought for a moment. He could have been angry, but instead, he found himself feeling sorry for the little chipmunk. "It's okay," he said softly. "I'll share my acorns with you. We can split them, so we both have enough for winter."

The chipmunk looked up, surprised. "Really? You'd do that?"

Max nodded. "We all need to help each other, especially when times are tough."

The chipmunk smiled, and together they divided the acorns. Max had learned a valuable lesson that day: sometimes, the best way to solve a problem is through understanding and kindness.

Max felt proud of himself. He had solved the mystery, and in doing so, he had made a new friend. Winter might be cold, but with friends by his side, Max knew he would be just fine.

Lessons Learned

1. Sometimes, people do things out of desperation, not malice.
2. It's important to look for understanding, even when you feel wronged.
3. Sharing with others in need can bring unexpected rewards.
4. Forgiveness is a powerful tool in building friendships.
5. Working together can help solve even the toughest problems.
6. True strength comes from kindness, not anger.
7. Helping others creates a sense of community and support.

Chapter 6: The Thunderstorm

The day had started out bright and sunny, with not a cloud in the sky. Max was enjoying a peaceful morning in the park, gathering acorns and watching the people stroll by. He had planned to spend the entire day outside, taking in the warmth of the sun. Luna, as usual, was flitting from tree to tree, offering cheerful commentary about the goings-on in the city.

But by the afternoon, the sky had changed. Dark clouds began to gather, and the once-gentle breeze turned into a gusty wind. Max looked up, his heart sinking. He had always hated storms. The rumbling of thunder and the sharp flashes of lightning made him feel uneasy, and worst of all, he hated getting wet. His fur would become matted and uncomfortable, and he'd be shivering for hours afterward.

As the first drops of rain began to fall, Max immediately started searching for shelter. He darted toward the nearest tree, but it was too exposed. The rain was picking up speed, and soon it was pouring down in thick sheets. Max spotted a bridge near the edge of the park and quickly scurried toward it, hoping to escape the worst of the storm.

By the time he reached the safety of the bridge, Max was already drenched. He shook himself off and huddled under the stone arch, watching as the rain turned the park into a muddy mess. His heart pounded in his chest as thunder rumbled ominously overhead. Max curled up tightly, trying to make himself as small as possible. This storm was much worse than he had anticipated.

Meanwhile, Luna had been flying high above when the storm rolled in. She loved the rain, and the wind gave her an extra boost as she soared through the sky. But when she realized that Max wasn't by her side, she quickly swooped down to look for him. It didn't take long for her to find him huddled under the bridge, looking miserable.

"Max!" Luna called out as she landed beside him. "What are you doing under here? The storm isn't that bad!"

THE ADVENTURE OF TRUE FRIENDSHIP IN THE BIG CITY

Max peeked out from under his paws, his fur soaked and sticking to his body. "It's terrible!" he said, his voice shaky. "I hate storms. The thunder, the lightning, the rain... I just want it to be over."

Luna smiled gently and shook the water from her feathers. "I know storms can be scary, but they don't have to be. You just have to learn to face them."

Max gave her a doubtful look. "Face them? How can you face something like this? The rain is awful, and the thunder—" He was interrupted by a loud clap of thunder, and he flinched, pressing himself closer to the wall of the bridge.

Luna hopped closer to him, her voice soft but encouraging. "Max, it's just a storm. It'll pass. And you're not alone—I'm here with you."

Max looked at Luna, feeling a small spark of comfort. It was true—he wasn't alone. Luna had been with him through other challenges, and somehow, things always seemed easier when she was around.

"I don't know, Luna," Max said, still unsure. "What if it gets worse?"

Luna thought for a moment, then smiled. "Why don't we face it together? Instead of hiding from the storm, let's step out into it and feel the rain. You might be surprised."

Max hesitated. The idea of stepping out into the rain was the last thing he wanted to do, but Luna's confidence was infectious. He trusted her, and maybe, just maybe, she was right.

"Okay," Max said reluctantly. "But only because you're with me."

Luna grinned. "That's the spirit! Come on, let's go."

Taking a deep breath, Max followed Luna out from under the bridge. The rain immediately soaked his fur again, and for a moment, he wanted to turn back. But Luna was beside him, her wings spread wide, enjoying the cool drops. She looked so at ease, and Max wanted to feel that way too.

They walked together through the park, the rain pouring down around them. At first, Max focused on how cold and wet he felt, but as they continued, something began to change. The rain wasn't so bad once he got used to it. In fact, it felt kind of refreshing. The air smelled fresh, and the sound of the raindrops hitting the leaves was soothing.

Luna laughed as she twirled in the air, letting the wind carry her. "See? It's not so bad, is it?"

Max gave a small smile. "I guess not. I mean, I'm still soaked, but... it's kind of nice in a way."

They walked for a while longer, and Max found himself paying less attention to the storm and more attention to the world around him. The trees glistened with droplets of water, and the usually busy park was quiet, giving them the space to enjoy the storm together.

When the thunder rumbled again, Max felt a shiver of fear, but Luna was right there, smiling at him. "It's just noise," she said. "Nothing to be afraid of."

Max nodded, feeling braver with Luna by his side. For the first time, he realized that storms, like all challenges, could be faced. And having a friend with him made all the difference.

As the storm began to pass, the rain slowed to a light drizzle, and the sun peeked through the clouds, casting a soft glow over the park. Max shook the water from his fur and looked at Luna, who was watching the sky with a contented expression.

"You know," Max said, "I never thought I'd say this, but I think I'm okay with storms now."

Luna chuckled. "See? You just needed a little help to face them."

Lessons Learned

1. Challenges are easier to face when you're not alone.
2. Sometimes, the things we fear are less scary once we confront them.
3. Stepping out of your comfort zone can lead to unexpected

discoveries.
4. Facing fears can make you stronger and more confident.
5. Having a friend by your side can turn a difficult situation into an adventure.
6. The storm will always pass, and things will get better.
7. Fear is a natural feeling, but it doesn't have to control you.

Chapter 7: The Great City Race

The buzz of excitement filled the park as animals from all over the city gathered for the annual Great City Race. It was one of the most anticipated events of the year, a friendly competition where birds and squirrels teamed up to race through the streets, parks, and rooftops of the city. Luna had participated in the race every year, and she was determined to win this time.

Max, however, was less enthusiastic. The idea of racing through the city, especially at such a fast pace, made him nervous. He wasn't particularly fast, and he didn't like the idea of competing in front of a crowd. But Luna had been so excited about the race that she had convinced Max to join her team.

"It's not about winning," Luna had said as they prepared for the race. "It's about having fun and challenging yourself. Besides, we'll be working together!"

Max had reluctantly agreed, but now, as he stood at the starting line, he wasn't so sure. The other teams looked fierce and ready to go, and Max felt a knot of anxiety form in his stomach.

Luna, on the other hand, was as confident as ever. She fluffed her feathers and gave Max an encouraging smile. "Just stick with me, Max. We'll do great!"

The starting whistle blew, and the race began. Birds soared into the air, and squirrels dashed along the ground, weaving through obstacles and leaping over barriers. Max hesitated for a moment, but Luna quickly nudged him forward.

"Come on, Max! We've got this!"

Max took off after Luna, trying to keep up as they darted through the city streets. At first, Max was overwhelmed by the speed and intensity of the race. The other teams were fast, and the course was filled with challenges—narrow alleys, tall fences, and even a stretch that went through a busy market.

THE ADVENTURE OF TRUE FRIENDSHIP IN THE BIG CITY

But Luna was always just ahead of him, guiding him through the obstacles with ease. She flew above, calling out directions and cheering Max on. "You're doing great, Max! Just keep going!"

As they ran, Max started to find his rhythm. The initial panic he had felt began to fade, and he focused on the path ahead. He wasn't the fastest, but he was determined to keep going. Luna's encouragement kept him motivated, and soon, he found himself enjoying the race.

They reached the halfway point, where the course led them up to the rooftops. Luna soared ahead, and Max followed, using the fire escapes and ledges to climb higher. The view from the top was breathtaking—the entire city stretched out before them, and for a moment, Max forgot they were in the middle of a race.

Luna landed beside him, her eyes sparkling. "Isn't this amazing? Look how far we've come!"

Max smiled, feeling a surge of pride. They were halfway through the race, and he hadn't given up. Luna had been right—it wasn't about winning. It was about pushing himself and having fun.

As they continued, Max found that he was enjoying the race more and more. He and Luna worked together as a team, helping each other over obstacles and laughing as they navigated the twists and turns of the city. The other teams were fast, but Max didn't mind. He was having fun, and that was all that mattered.

By the time they reached the finish line, Max was exhausted but happy. They didn't win the race, but they had finished together, and that was a victory in itself.

"Great job, Max!" Luna said, beaming. "I'm so proud of you!"

Max grinned, feeling a sense of accomplishment he hadn't expected. The Great City Race had been a challenge, but with Luna's support, he had faced it head-on. And in the end, it wasn't about winning—it was about the experience, the fun, and the friendship. The city looked completely different at night. The hustle and bustle of the day gave way to a quieter, more mysterious atmosphere. The streets were lit by the soft glow of streetlights, and the usually busy parks were still and peaceful. It was a world Max had never really seen, as he was usually nestled in his tree long before the sun went down.

But tonight was different. Luna had invited him on a special midnight adventure, and though Max was hesitant, he had agreed. Luna always had a way of making things sound exciting, and she had promised that exploring the city at night was an experience unlike any other.

Lessons Learned

1. Healthy competition is about doing your best, not just winning.
2. Encouragement from a friend can help you push through challenges.
3. It's okay to feel nervous, but don't let fear stop you from trying new things.
4. Working as a team can make difficult tasks more enjoyable.
5. Sometimes the journey is more important than the destination.
6. You don't have to be the fastest or the best to feel proud of your efforts.
7. True success comes from trying your best and enjoying the process.

Chapter 8: The Midnight Adventure

As they set out, Max couldn't help but feel a little nervous. The shadows seemed longer, and the unfamiliar sounds of the night filled the air. But Luna was as calm and confident as ever, gliding effortlessly through the darkened streets.

"Don't worry, Max," she said, her voice soft but reassuring. "The city may look different at night, but it's still the same place. You just have to learn to see it in a new way."

Max nodded, trying to push his fears aside. He trusted Luna, and if she thought this was worth exploring, then he would give it a try.

They started their adventure by visiting some of Luna's favorite spots. The first stop was a quiet park near the river, where the moonlight shimmered on the water's surface. Max had never seen the city this way—so peaceful and calm. The usually busy streets were almost empty, and the soft sounds of the night created a soothing backdrop.

As they walked, Max began to relax. The night wasn't as scary as he had imagined. In fact, there was something magical about the way the city looked under the moonlight.

"See?" Luna said with a smile. "The night has its own kind of beauty."

Max agreed. The city felt different, but in a good way. It was like discovering a whole new world, one that was quiet and full of mystery.

Their next stop was the rooftop of a tall building, where they could see the entire city spread out before them. The lights twinkled like stars, and Max felt a sense of awe as he took it all in.

"This is incredible," Max said, his fear completely gone now. "I never knew the city could look like this."

Luna grinned. "That's the thing about adventures, Max. They show you things you never knew existed."

As they continued their midnight journey, Max realized that the city at night wasn't something to be afraid of—it was something to be explored and appreciated. With Luna by his side, he felt brave, even in the face of the unknown.

By the time they returned to the park, Max felt a sense of accomplishment. He had faced his fear of the dark and discovered a new side of the city that he had never seen before.

"I'm glad we did this," Max said, smiling at Luna. "I was scared at first, but now I see how beautiful the night can be."

Luna nodded. "I knew you'd love it. Sometimes, all it takes is a little courage to see things in a new way."

Max realized that this midnight adventure had taught him more than just how to appreciate the night—it had shown him the importance of trusting his instincts, being brave, and embracing the unfamiliar. Max and Luna had been exploring the city for weeks now, and with each new adventure, they grew closer as friends. But today, they stumbled upon something neither of them had expected—a hidden, old library in the middle of the city.

They had been wandering through a quiet part of town, far from the busy streets and tall buildings, when they noticed a crumbling brick building covered in ivy. The windows were dusty, and the door was slightly ajar, as if no one had entered in years.

"Do you think we should go in?" Max asked, peering through the open door. The dim light inside revealed rows and rows of old books, their spines worn and faded.

Luna's eyes lit up. "Absolutely! Who knows what kind of treasures we'll find in there?"

Max hesitated for a moment, but his curiosity got the better of him. He followed Luna inside, and together they stepped into the dusty, quiet library.

THE ADVENTURE OF TRUE FRIENDSHIP IN THE BIG CITY

The air smelled of old paper and forgotten history, and Max felt a sense of awe as he looked around. The shelves were packed with books of all sizes and colors, and the room seemed to stretch on forever.

"This place is amazing," Max whispered. "I didn't even know libraries like this existed."

Luna nodded, her eyes wide with excitement. "Me neither! I wonder what kind of stories are hidden in these books."

Lessons Learned

1. New experiences can help you see familiar places in a different light.
2. Facing your fears can lead to unexpected discoveries.
3. Trusting a friend can give you the courage to try new things.
4. The unknown isn't always scary—it can be full of wonder and beauty.
5. Nighttime has its own magic, if you're willing to explore it.
6. Being brave doesn't mean you're not scared—it means trying anyway.
7. True adventures often begin when you step outside of your comfort zone.

Chapter 9: The Old Library

They spent hours exploring the library, pulling books off the shelves and reading passages aloud. Max found an old map of the city, showing streets and buildings that no longer existed. Luna discovered a collection of poems that had been written by animals from long ago.

As they explored, Max realized how much knowledge was stored in these books. Each one held a piece of history, a story, or a lesson just waiting to be discovered.

"I've never been much of a reader," Max admitted as he flipped through an old book about the city's history. "But this is… different. It's like we're uncovering a secret world."

Luna smiled. "That's the power of books, Max. They open up new worlds and let you see things you never imagined."

By the time they left the library, Max felt inspired. He had learned so much in just a few hours, and he couldn't wait to come back and explore more.

"That was one of the best adventures yet," Max said as they walked back to the park. "I had no idea books could be so… exciting."

Luna nodded in agreement. "Books are full of possibilities, Max. And the best part? There's always something new to learn."

Max realized that the old library had taught him more than just facts about the city—it had shown him the value of curiosity, discovery, and the endless possibilities that came with learning.

The city market was unlike anything Max had ever experienced. It was a bustling, colorful place filled with animals from all over the world, each one offering something unique—fruits, vegetables, spices, and trinkets that Max had never seen before. Luna had talked about the market for weeks, and today she had finally convinced Max to come along.

At first, Max felt overwhelmed. The sights, sounds, and smells were all so different from the quiet park he was used to. The market was loud,

THE ADVENTURE OF TRUE FRIENDSHIP IN THE BIG CITY 31

with animals calling out to one another in different languages, and the variety of foods and goods was dizzying.

But Luna was right at home. She flitted from stall to stall, chatting with vendors and picking out snacks to share with Max. "Try this," she said, handing him a small, brightly colored fruit. "It's from the other side of the city. It's delicious!"

Max hesitated but took a bite. The sweet, tangy flavor burst in his mouth, and he smiled. "That's amazing! I've never tasted anything like it."

Luna grinned. "There's so much to explore here, Max. Every corner of the city has something new to offer."

As they wandered through the market, Max began to appreciate the diversity around him. Each stall offered something different, and every animal had a unique story to tell. Some had traveled from faraway places, bringing with them foods and goods that Max had never even heard of.

"This market is like a little piece of the whole world," Max said as they passed a stall selling colorful fabrics from distant lands.

Luna nodded. "Exactly! And that's what makes it so special. It's a place where everyone comes together, sharing what they have and learning from one another."

Max realized that the market wasn't just a place to buy things—it was a place where animals from different backgrounds came together to celebrate their differences and share their cultures.

By the time they left, Max felt a new sense of appreciation for the diversity of the city. He had tasted foods he'd never imagined, heard languages he didn't understand, and met animals from all walks of life. And through it all, he had learned that differences weren't something to be afraid of—they were something to celebrate.

"That was incredible," Max said as they walked back to the park. "I never knew the city was so... diverse."

Luna smiled. "That's the beauty of the market, Max. It shows you that even though we're all different, we're all part of the same community."

Max nodded, feeling grateful for the experience. The market had taught him that diversity wasn't just about the foods or goods that animals brought to the market—it was about the connections they made and the stories they shared.

Lessons Learned

1. Diversity makes a community richer and more vibrant.
2. Differences should be celebrated, not feared.
3. Trying new things can open your mind to new possibilities.
4. Every culture has something valuable to offer.
5. Connecting with others helps build a stronger, more understanding community.
6. The world is full of unique experiences waiting to be explored.
7. Sharing and learning from others brings people closer together.

Chapter 10: The Art of Flying

Max had always believed that squirrels were meant to stay on the ground, or at least on the branches of trees. Flying was for birds like Luna, who could soar through the sky with grace and ease. He was perfectly content to scamper from tree to tree, using his nimble paws to dart through the forest. But Luna had different ideas.

One day, as they wandered through the park, Luna looked down from a tall oak tree where she had landed and said, "Max, have you ever thought about flying?"

Max looked up at her, incredulous. "Flying? You mean with wings? Luna, I'm a squirrel. I don't have wings."

Luna laughed and shook her head. "No, not with wings! But you can glide, can't you? I've seen squirrels leap from tree to tree, catching the air just right. It's not exactly flying, but it's pretty close."

Max considered this for a moment. He had made leaps between branches before, but he had never thought of it as anything like flying. It was just what squirrels did. Still, the idea intrigued him. He had always admired the way Luna could take to the skies so effortlessly, and a part of him wondered what it might feel like to experience even a fraction of that freedom.

"I guess I've never really tried to glide like you're talking about," Max admitted. "But I'm not sure it's something I'm cut out for."

Luna flitted down from the tree and landed beside him, her eyes gleaming with excitement. "Nonsense! You're perfectly capable. You've just never given it a proper shot. Come on, let's find a good tree to start with."

Before Max could protest, Luna was already leading him to the tallest tree in the park. Max's heart began to race as he looked up at the high branches. This was much higher than the trees he was used to. He suddenly felt very small.

"Uh, Luna… I'm not sure this is such a good idea," Max said, taking a step back.

Luna fluttered back down and gave him a reassuring nudge. "Trust me, Max. I'll be right here with you. We'll start small, and if it doesn't work out, at least you'll know you gave it a try. Besides, you're braver than you think."

Max took a deep breath and nodded. Luna was right—he had faced bigger challenges before. This was just one more new thing to try. With a burst of determination, Max scampered up the tree trunk, reaching a sturdy branch about halfway up.

"Okay, what now?" Max called down to Luna, who had perched on a branch beside him.

"Now you leap!" Luna said with a grin. "You'll catch the wind and glide over to that branch there."

Max glanced at the branch Luna was pointing to. It didn't look too far away, but the gap between the trees suddenly seemed wider than it had from the ground. Still, Max braced himself and took a deep breath.

He leaped.

For a brief moment, Max felt the rush of air beneath him. His heart soared as he hung in the air, and for the first time, he understood what Luna meant about gliding. But just as quickly, gravity took over, and Max tumbled to the ground in a flurry of paws and fur.

Luna swooped down beside him, stifling a laugh. "You almost had it! You just need to catch the wind better next time."

Max shook himself off, his pride more bruised than his body. "Almost? I didn't even come close!"

"Don't give up yet!" Luna said, offering him a wing to help him up. "You're still learning. It's all about timing and trust. You'll get the hang of it."

Max sighed but nodded. Luna wasn't going to let him quit, and deep down, he didn't want to. He wanted to know what it felt like to glide, to move through the air with the kind of freedom Luna experienced every day.

They tried again. And again. Each time, Max got a little closer, staying airborne for just a fraction longer. But each time, he found himself back on the ground, frustrated but determined. Luna remained patient, offering tips and encouragement at every turn.

Hours passed, and just when Max thought he couldn't keep going, something clicked. He took a running leap off the branch, and this time, instead of falling straight down, he caught the wind just right. For a few glorious seconds, Max was gliding. It wasn't the same as flying, but it was close enough. The feeling of weightlessness, the breeze rushing past him—it was exhilarating.

He landed on the next branch, his heart pounding with excitement. "I did it!" Max shouted, his voice filled with disbelief.

Luna cheered from below, her wings flapping with joy. "I knew you could do it!"

Max grinned from ear to ear. He couldn't believe it—he had actually glided from one tree to another. The thrill of trying something new and succeeding, even after failing so many times, filled him with a sense of pride he hadn't expected.

Lessons Learned

1. Trying new things can lead to surprising discoveries about yourself.
2. Perseverance is key when learning something new, even when it feels impossible at first.
3. Trusting the process is important—improvement often comes slowly.
4. Friends can encourage you to step outside your comfort zone and help you succeed.
5. Even if you fail at first, keep trying—you might get better with practice.

6. Facing fears can lead to thrilling new experiences.
7. It's okay to struggle; what matters is that you keep going.

Chapter 11: The Friendship Festival

The annual Friendship Festival was one of the biggest events in the city. Animals from every corner of the park, the rooftops, and even the outskirts of town gathered to celebrate the bonds of friendship. There were games, performances, dances, and food stalls offering treats from all over. It was a day full of joy, laughter, and the spirit of togetherness.

This year, Luna was especially excited. She had convinced Max to attend the festival with her, and though Max wasn't a huge fan of large crowds, he couldn't deny Luna's enthusiasm. As they made their way to the festival grounds, Max couldn't help but feel a sense of anticipation building.

"Wait until you see the games, Max!" Luna said, practically bouncing with excitement. "There's one where you have to work together to solve puzzles, and another where you race across obstacle courses with a partner. It's all about teamwork and having fun!"

Max smiled at her enthusiasm. He had never been to a festival before, and while he wasn't sure what to expect, Luna's excitement was contagious.

As they arrived at the festival grounds, Max's eyes widened at the sight before him. The park had been transformed into a vibrant, bustling space filled with color and music. Banners fluttered in the breeze, and animals of all kinds—squirrels, pigeons, rabbits, mice, even foxes—were milling about, laughing and chatting as they enjoyed the festivities.

"Come on, Max! Let's start with the games!" Luna urged, pulling him toward a large open field where animals were already gathering for the first event.

The first game was a team obstacle course, where pairs of animals had to work together to navigate a series of challenges. Max and Luna were paired up, and as the race began, Max felt a burst of determination. He had never been the fastest or the strongest, but with Luna by his side, he knew they could do anything.

The course was full of tricky obstacles—climbing over logs, jumping across streams, and weaving through a maze of bushes. Max and Luna worked together, cheering each other on as they tackled each challenge. Luna, with her ability to fly, helped Max over the taller obstacles, while Max used his agility to guide them through the tighter spaces.

By the time they reached the finish line, they were both out of breath but beaming with pride. They hadn't won the race, but that didn't matter. What mattered was the fun they'd had and the way they had worked together as a team.

"That was amazing, Max!" Luna said, her feathers ruffled from the excitement. "You were incredible!"

Max grinned, his heart swelling with pride. "We made a great team."

Next, they moved on to the puzzle-solving challenge. In this game, pairs of animals had to work together to solve a series of riddles and puzzles, unlocking clues that would lead them to the final solution. Max wasn't sure how good he would be at solving puzzles, but Luna was confident they could figure it out.

The puzzles were tough—some required clever thinking, while others involved careful observation and attention to detail. But Max and Luna quickly found their rhythm, combining their skills to crack each riddle. Max's patience and analytical mind complemented Luna's quick thinking and creativity, and together they breezed through the challenge.

By the end of the puzzle game, Max was feeling more confident than ever. He had never realized how much fun it could be to work together with a friend to solve problems and face challenges. The Friendship Festival was turning out to be a day of discovery, not just about the games, but about the strength of their friendship.

THE ADVENTURE OF TRUE FRIENDSHIP IN THE BIG CITY

After a full day of games and laughter, the sun began to set, and the festival ended with a grand dance. Animals gathered in the clearing, and music filled the air as everyone joined in the celebration. Luna, always full of energy, dragged Max onto the dance floor, and though he was a little shy at first, Max soon found himself swept up in the rhythm of the music.

Lessons Learned

1. Friendship is something worth celebrating.
2. Working together with a friend can make challenges more fun and rewarding.
3. Teamwork strengthens the bond between friends.
4. Celebrating friendships brings joy to life.
5. Every friendship is unique and valuable in its own way.
6. Sharing experiences, whether winning or losing, deepens connections.
7. The best memories are often made with friends by your side.

Chapter 12: The Hidden Tunnel

It was a quiet morning in the park when Luna excitedly flew down to where Max was lounging under his favorite tree. Her eyes sparkled with excitement, and Max could tell right away that she had something planned.

"Max, you'll never believe what I found!" Luna exclaimed, practically bouncing on her feet. "There's this hidden tunnel under the city, and I think it leads to a secret garden!"

Max sat up, curious but skeptical. "A secret garden? That sounds a little far-fetched, don't you think?"

Luna grinned, undeterred. "It may sound crazy, but I heard it from one of the older pigeons. They said the tunnel's been there for years, but no one's explored it in a long time. I think we should check it out!"

Max hesitated. He wasn't particularly fond of dark, enclosed spaces, and the idea of venturing into an underground tunnel didn't exactly thrill him. But Luna had a way of making every adventure sound exciting, and Max couldn't help but be drawn in by her enthusiasm.

"I don't know, Luna," Max said slowly. "Tunnels can be dangerous. What if we get lost?"

Luna waved a wing dismissively. "We won't get lost! I have a good sense of direction, and besides, I've already scouted the entrance. It's not too far from here."

Max sighed, knowing that once Luna set her mind on something, there was no stopping her. And truth be told, a part of him was curious. The idea of discovering a secret garden hidden away under the city was intriguing, even if it meant facing his fear of dark, enclosed spaces.

"All right," Max said finally. "Let's do it. But if we get lost, I'm blaming you."

Luna laughed and gave him a playful nudge. "Deal! Come on, the tunnel's this way."

They made their way through the park and into the city, weaving through streets and alleyways until they reached a small, overgrown lot behind an old building. There, hidden beneath a pile of leaves and debris, was the entrance to the tunnel—an old, crumbling stone archway that led into the darkness below.

Max's heart raced as he peered into the tunnel. It was dark, damp, and the air smelled of earth and old stone. He took a deep breath, trying to steady his nerves.

Luna, on the other hand, seemed completely unfazed. She fluttered down to the entrance and looked back at Max with a reassuring smile. "Ready?"

Max swallowed his fear and nodded. "Ready."

They entered the tunnel, the light from the entrance quickly fading behind them as they ventured deeper into the underground passage. The walls were cool and rough, and the sound of their footsteps echoed in the narrow space. Max's fur prickled with unease, but he kept going, trusting Luna to lead the way.

As they walked, the tunnel began to twist and turn, and Max started to lose his sense of direction. The air grew colder, and every sound seemed amplified in the stillness. Max's imagination ran wild with thoughts of getting lost or encountering something dangerous in the darkness.

"Are you sure we're going the right way?" Max asked nervously.

Luna, who was a few steps ahead, nodded confidently. "We're almost there. I can feel it."

Max wasn't so sure, but he trusted Luna's instincts. They had been through plenty of adventures together, and Luna had never led him astray.

After what felt like hours of walking, the tunnel suddenly opened up into a larger chamber. The ceiling was higher, and light filtered in from small cracks above, illuminating the space. Max gasped as he looked around.

In the center of the chamber was a small garden, overgrown but still beautiful. Flowers of all colors bloomed in the soft light, and vines climbed the walls, creating a lush, hidden oasis in the middle of the underground space.

Luna beamed. "I told you there was a secret garden!"

Max couldn't believe his eyes. The garden was more beautiful than he had imagined. It was peaceful, quiet, and untouched by the hustle and bustle of the city above.

They spent hours exploring the garden, discovering all kinds of hidden corners and rare plants. Max even found a small stream running through the center of the chamber, its water clear and cool. It was like stepping into another world, far removed from the noise and chaos of the city.

As they sat by the stream, Max felt a sense of calm wash over him. The journey through the tunnel had been nerve-wracking, but the reward was more than worth it.

"I'm glad we came," Max admitted, smiling at Luna. "This place is amazing."

Luna nodded, her eyes shining with satisfaction. "I knew you'd love it. Sometimes the best things are hidden away, and you have to take a little risk to find them."

Max realized that Luna was right. Facing his fear of the dark and the unknown had led him to something beautiful, something he never would have discovered if he had stayed in his comfort zone. The hidden tunnel had been a challenge, but it had also been an adventure—and one he was glad he hadn't missed.

Lessons Learned

1. Facing your fears can lead to unexpected rewards.
2. Sometimes the best discoveries are hidden in unlikely places.
3. Trusting a friend can help you overcome doubts and challenges.

THE ADVENTURE OF TRUE FRIENDSHIP IN THE BIG CITY

4. Exploration requires a willingness to step into the unknown.
5. Taking risks can lead to beautiful new experiences.
6. Adventure is about the journey as much as the destination.
7. Courage is found in trying, even when you're afraid.

Chapter 13: The Concert in Central Park

Max had never been much for music. Sure, he enjoyed the occasional chirp of birds in the trees or the rustling of leaves in the wind, but organized music—especially the kind with instruments—was something he had never really paid much attention to. Luna, on the other hand, loved music. She was always humming a tune or tapping her feet to a rhythm only she could hear.

So when Luna invited Max to a special concert in Central Park, Max wasn't sure what to expect. The idea of sitting still and listening to music for hours didn't exactly sound like his idea of fun, but Luna had insisted that it would be an experience he wouldn't want to miss.

"It's not just any concert, Max," Luna had explained. "Animals from all over the city come to perform, and it's unlike anything you've ever heard before. Trust me, you'll love it."

Max had reluctantly agreed, though he was still skeptical. But as they arrived at the open-air concert venue in the heart of Central Park, Max was immediately struck by the atmosphere. The sun was setting, casting a warm glow over the trees, and animals of all kinds were gathering in the clearing, chatting excitedly as they found spots to sit.

The stage was set up at the far end of the clearing, adorned with twinkling lights and surrounded by lush greenery. Instruments of all shapes and sizes were arranged on the stage—drums, flutes, strings, and even a large set of chimes that glistened in the evening light.

"Wow," Max said, his skepticism fading as he took in the scene. "This is... different."

Luna grinned. "Just wait until the music starts. You're going to love it."

They found a spot near the front of the crowd and settled in as the musicians took their places on stage. Max noticed animals from all over the city—rabbits, foxes, owls, and even a few raccoons—each holding an instrument and preparing to play. It was clear that this concert was a big deal, and the performers were excited to share their music.

As the first notes filled the air, Max felt a strange sensation wash over him. The music was soft at first, a gentle melody that seemed to flow through the trees and across the grass. The sound of the flute blended with the strings, creating a harmony that was both soothing and uplifting.

Max closed his eyes, letting the music wash over him. He could hear the rhythm of the drums, the delicate plucking of strings, and the haunting call of the flute. It was unlike anything he had ever experienced before. The music seemed to tell a story, painting pictures in his mind of far-off places, peaceful meadows, and starry nights.

As the concert continued, Max found himself tapping his paw to the rhythm, completely absorbed in the music. He had never realized how powerful music could be, how it could make him feel so many different emotions all at once. There were moments when the music made him feel light and joyful, as if he were soaring through the sky, and other moments when the melody turned somber, filling him with a sense of longing and reflection.

Luna watched Max with a smile, clearly pleased that he was enjoying the concert. "I told you music was amazing," she whispered during a brief pause between songs.

Max nodded, still in awe of what he was hearing. "I had no idea music could be like this," he admitted. "It's... incredible."

The final piece of the concert was a grand symphony, performed by the entire ensemble. The music swelled and filled the air with a sense of grandeur and triumph, and as the last note echoed through the park, the crowd erupted in applause.

Max joined in, clapping his paws together with enthusiasm. He had been completely captivated by the performance, and for the first time in his life, he truly understood the magic of music.

As the concert ended and the crowd began to disperse, Max and Luna lingered in the clearing, still caught up in the beauty of the evening.

"That was one of the most incredible things I've ever experienced," Max said, his voice filled with wonder. "I can't believe I almost didn't come."

Luna smiled warmly. "Music has a way of touching your heart, even when you don't expect it. It's one of the most creative ways to express yourself and connect with others."

Max nodded, thinking about how the music had made him feel. It had been like a conversation without words, a way of sharing emotions and stories that he couldn't have understood any other way.

"I get it now," Max said thoughtfully. "Music isn't just sound. It's... feeling."

Luna's eyes sparkled with understanding. "Exactly. And the best part is, there's always more to discover. Every song, every melody, has its own story to tell."

Lessons Learned

1. Music is a powerful way to express emotions and tell stories.
2. Trying something new can open your mind to unexpected joys.
3. Creative expression comes in many forms, and each is valuable in its own way.
4. You don't have to be an expert to appreciate the beauty of music.
5. Sharing experiences with friends can deepen your understanding of the world.
6. Music has the ability to connect people and create shared moments of joy.
7. It's important to be open to new experiences, even if they're outside your comfort zone.

Chapter 14: The Mischievous Monkey

Max and Luna were enjoying a peaceful afternoon in the park when they heard a loud crash coming from the direction of the market. Curious, they hurried over to see what was going on. When they arrived, they found a scene of chaos—fruits and vegetables were scattered across the ground, and animals were rushing to pick up the mess.

In the middle of it all was a small monkey, swinging from a lamppost with a mischievous grin on his face. He was clearly the cause of the commotion, and he seemed to be enjoying every moment of it.

"What's going on?" Max asked a nearby squirrel, who was frantically trying to gather the spilled food.

"That monkey's been causing trouble all week," the squirrel replied, exasperated. "He's always stealing food and knocking things over. No one knows what to do with him."

Luna narrowed her eyes, watching the monkey as he swung from one lamppost to another, clearly enjoying the chaos he was creating. "We need to do something about this," she said, determined.

Max wasn't so sure. "What can we do? He's causing so much trouble, and it doesn't look like he's going to stop anytime soon."

Luna thought for a moment, her brow furrowed in concentration. "Maybe he's not trying to be bad. Maybe he's just bored or doesn't know how to ask for help."

Max wasn't convinced. "He's stealing food and making a mess. How can we help someone who's causing so much trouble?"

But Luna was already on the move, flying up to where the monkey was swinging. "Hey there!" she called out, her voice calm but firm. "What are you up to?"

The monkey stopped mid-swing and looked at Luna, clearly surprised that someone was addressing him directly. "Just having some fun," he replied with a shrug, still hanging from the lamppost.

Luna perched on a nearby branch, her tone gentle but serious. "It looks like your fun is causing problems for everyone else. How about we figure out a better way for you to enjoy yourself without making such a mess?"

The monkey frowned, clearly not expecting Luna to approach the situation this way. "What do you mean? I'm just playing around."

Max, who had been watching from below, stepped forward cautiously. "It's not just about playing. You're taking things that don't belong to you and making it harder for everyone else. Maybe there's a better way to have fun without causing trouble."

The monkey seemed to consider this for a moment, his mischievous grin fading slightly. "I guess... I didn't really think about it that way."

Luna smiled, her voice kind. "We all get bored or restless sometimes, but there are other ways to have fun. Maybe we can help you find something that's exciting without causing so much trouble."

Max nodded, stepping up beside Luna. "What if we showed you some games we play in the park? You might find them more fun than knocking over food stalls."

The monkey looked intrigued. "Games? What kind of games?"

Luna's eyes lit up. "We play all sorts of things! Races, puzzles, climbing challenges—things that are just as exciting but don't cause so much chaos."

The monkey's expression softened, and he swung down from the lamppost, landing gracefully on the ground. "Okay," he said slowly. "I'll give it a try."

Max and Luna spent the rest of the afternoon showing the monkey how to play different games in the park. They raced through the trees, played hide-and-seek, and even set up an obstacle course for him to swing through. The monkey quickly got the hang of it, and for the first time, Max saw him smiling and laughing without causing any trouble.

THE ADVENTURE OF TRUE FRIENDSHIP IN THE BIG CITY

By the end of the day, the monkey seemed happier and more relaxed than he had when they first met. "Thanks," he said as they sat down to rest. "I didn't realize there were other ways to have fun."

Luna smiled warmly. "Sometimes we just need to find the right outlet for our energy. There's always a better way to enjoy yourself without hurting others."

Max nodded in agreement. "And if you ever feel bored or restless again, just come find us. We're always up for a game."

The monkey grinned, clearly grateful for the new friends he had made. "I think I will."

The mischievous monkey had turned out to be more playful than malicious, and with a little patience and understanding, they had helped him discover a new way to have fun.

Lessons Learned

1. Sometimes, people act out because they don't know a better way to express themselves.
2. Patience and understanding can help resolve conflicts.
3. Offering solutions is often more effective than criticizing someone's behavior.
4. Playfulness and energy can be channeled into positive activities.
5. Helping others find better outlets for their behavior can lead to new friendships.
6. Problem-solving requires creativity and empathy.
7. Everyone deserves a chance to learn and grow, even if they've made mistakes.

Chapter 15: The City Marathon

The City Marathon was one of the biggest events of the year. Animals from all corners of the city gathered to participate in the race, which wound through busy streets, parks, alleys, and even over rooftops. It was a test of endurance, speed, and teamwork, and it attracted competitors of all kinds—birds, squirrels, mice, rabbits, and even a few energetic raccoons.

Max had never considered himself much of a runner, but when Luna suggested they enter the marathon as a team, he couldn't resist the challenge. Luna, with her boundless energy and enthusiasm, was confident that they would make a great pair. Max wasn't so sure—he wasn't known for his speed or stamina—but Luna's excitement was contagious, and he agreed to give it a try.

The morning of the marathon was bright and cool, with a light breeze rustling the leaves in the park. Max and Luna arrived at the starting line, where a large crowd of animals had already gathered. The atmosphere was electric, filled with anticipation and excitement. Some animals were warming up, stretching their legs and wings, while others chatted nervously, comparing strategies for the race.

"Are you ready, Max?" Luna asked, bouncing on her toes with excitement. "This is going to be amazing!"

Max took a deep breath, feeling the nervous energy in his chest. "I think so," he said, trying to sound more confident than he felt. "I'm just hoping I can keep up with you."

Luna grinned and gave him a reassuring pat on the back. "Don't worry! This isn't about winning—it's about pushing ourselves and working together. We'll be fine as long as we stick together."

Max nodded, feeling a bit more at ease. Luna always had a way of calming his nerves, and her enthusiasm made him believe that maybe, just maybe, they could finish the race.

THE ADVENTURE OF TRUE FRIENDSHIP IN THE BIG CITY

As the starting whistle blew, the crowd surged forward, and the marathon began. Max and Luna started off at a steady pace, weaving through the crowd as they made their way down the wide city streets. The first part of the course was relatively easy, with flat roads and plenty of space to run. Max felt a surge of confidence as they passed a few other teams, keeping a comfortable rhythm with Luna by his side.

"This isn't so bad," Max said, glancing at Luna. "We're doing great!"

Luna smiled, her wings fluttering slightly as she kept pace with him. "Just wait until we hit the park trails! That's where things get interesting."

Sure enough, as they entered the park, the terrain became more challenging. The smooth city streets gave way to dirt paths, twisting through trees and over small hills. The ground was uneven, and Max had to watch his step carefully to avoid tripping on roots and rocks. His legs were starting to burn, but he pushed through, determined to keep going.

Luna, as usual, was full of energy, darting ahead and then circling back to encourage Max. "You're doing great! Just keep moving—don't worry about the others."

Max appreciated her support, but he could feel the fatigue starting to set in. They were only halfway through the marathon, and the toughest parts were still ahead. He glanced around and saw other teams starting to slow down as well—some animals were panting heavily, while others were stopping to rest in the shade.

As they approached a particularly steep hill, Max felt his confidence waver. His legs were aching, and his breath was coming in short, ragged bursts. "Luna... I don't know if I can make it up this hill," he panted.

Luna, hovering just ahead of him, turned back with a determined look in her eyes. "You can do it, Max! Just take it one step at a time. I'm right here with you."

Max gritted his teeth and kept moving, focusing on putting one paw in front of the other. The hill seemed to stretch on forever, and with each step, his legs felt heavier. But Luna's constant encouragement kept him going. She flew beside him, offering words of support and occasionally nudging him forward when he started to slow down.

Finally, after what felt like an eternity, they reached the top of the hill. Max collapsed onto the grass, gasping for breath, while Luna landed beside him with a triumphant smile.

"You did it!" Luna said, her voice full of pride. "I knew you could."

Max smiled weakly, still trying to catch his breath. "I don't think I've ever been this tired in my life."

Luna chuckled and nudged him playfully. "You're stronger than you think, Max. You just proved that."

After a short rest, they continued on their way, the hardest part of the course now behind them. As they ran through the final stretch of the marathon, the city streets once again opened up, and Max could see the finish line in the distance. His heart lifted at the sight—despite the fatigue, despite the challenges, they were almost there.

As they approached the finish line, Max felt a surge of energy. He glanced at Luna, who was smiling brightly, and together they pushed forward, crossing the line side by side. The crowd cheered as they finished, and Max couldn't help but feel a sense of pride and accomplishment.

"We did it," Max said, his chest heaving with exertion but his face lit up with a smile.

Luna beamed at him. "I told you we could! You were amazing, Max. I'm so proud of you."

Max felt a warmth in his chest, not just from finishing the marathon, but from the support and teamwork that had carried them through. It hadn't been easy, but they had done it together, and that made the victory even sweeter.

THE ADVENTURE OF TRUE FRIENDSHIP IN THE BIG CITY

As they rested in the park after the race, Max reflected on the experience. The marathon had been a test of endurance and determination, but it had also been a lesson in teamwork. He had relied on Luna's support to keep going when things got tough, and together they had achieved something they wouldn't have been able to do alone.

"Thanks for believing in me, Luna," Max said, his voice soft but sincere. "I couldn't have done this without you."

Luna smiled warmly and gave him a gentle nudge. "We did this together, Max. That's what teamwork is all about."

Lessons Learned

1. Endurance is about pushing through challenges, even when they seem overwhelming.
2. Teamwork makes difficult tasks easier and more rewarding.
3. Encouragement from a friend can give you the strength to keep going.
4. Success isn't just about reaching the finish line—it's about the journey and the effort you put in.
5. Challenges are easier to overcome when you face them with someone you trust.
6. Everyone has more strength than they realize—it often takes a challenge to discover it.
7. Achieving a goal with a friend is more meaningful than achieving it alone.

Chapter 16: The Winter's Tale

As the days grew shorter and the air turned colder, Max could feel the change in the city. The vibrant energy of summer and fall gave way to the stillness of winter, and the animals of the city began to prepare for the long, cold months ahead. For Max, winter meant one thing: hibernation. It was a time for him to retreat to his cozy nest and sleep through the coldest part of the year, storing up energy until the warmth of spring returned.

But this year, something was different. This year, Max had Luna.

Max had never had a friend like Luna before, and the thought of spending months without her filled him with a sense of unease. He wasn't sure how he would cope with being away from her for so long. They had spent so much time together, sharing adventures and exploring the city, that the idea of not seeing her every day made him feel strangely anxious.

One crisp morning, as Max and Luna sat in their favorite spot in the park, Max finally brought up his concerns.

"Luna, winter's almost here," Max said, his voice quiet. "And... well, I'll be hibernating soon."

Luna, perched on a branch above him, tilted her head curiously. "Hibernating? You mean you're going to sleep for the whole winter?"

Max nodded. "That's what squirrels do. We gather food, make our nests cozy, and sleep until spring. I won't be able to see you for a while."

Luna frowned, her feathers ruffling slightly. "I didn't realize it would be that long. How long will you be gone?"

"Months," Max replied, his ears drooping slightly. "I'll wake up when the weather gets warmer, but until then…"

Luna fluttered down to sit beside him, her eyes filled with understanding. "I'll miss you, Max. But I understand—it's what you need to do."

Max looked down at his paws, feeling a pang of sadness. "I don't want to leave you, though. I've never had a friend like you before."

Luna smiled gently and placed a wing on his shoulder. "We'll still be friends, Max. Even if we can't see each other for a while, our friendship won't go away. It'll still be there when you wake up."

Max nodded, though the thought of being apart from Luna still weighed on his mind. "I just... I don't want things to change."

Luna's eyes softened, and she gave him a reassuring look. "Change is a part of life, Max. But it doesn't have to be a bad thing. Winter will come and go, and when it's over, we'll pick up right where we left off. You don't have to worry about losing me."

Max sighed, feeling a little better but still uncertain. "I guess you're right. It's just... new for me."

Over the next few weeks, Max and Luna prepared for the coming winter. Max gathered acorns and other supplies, carefully storing them in his nest. Luna helped him, flying back and forth with small bundles of food, and together they made sure Max's nest was as cozy and well-stocked as possible.

As they worked, Max began to realize that Luna was right—change wasn't necessarily a bad thing. Yes, winter would be different, but it didn't mean the end of their friendship. It just meant they would have to adapt, and when spring came, they would have more adventures to look forward to.

On the last day before Max was set to begin his hibernation, Luna flew down to his nest with a small gift—a brightly colored feather from her own wing.

"I want you to keep this," Luna said, placing the feather in Max's nest. "That way, even while you're hibernating, you'll have a little reminder of me."

Max smiled, touched by the gesture. "Thanks, Luna. I'll keep it safe."

Luna nodded, her expression warm but a little sad. "And when you wake up, the first thing we'll do is go on a new adventure. Deal?"

Max's heart lifted at the thought. "Deal."

That night, as Max settled into his cozy nest, surrounded by the food he had carefully gathered, he looked at the bright feather Luna had given him. He felt a sense of peace wash over him, knowing that their friendship was strong enough to withstand the long winter ahead.

And with that thought in mind, Max drifted off to sleep, ready to face the winter and whatever changes it might bring.

As the months passed and the snow fell softly over the city, Luna continued her daily routines, often thinking of Max and the adventures they would have when spring returned. She flew over the park, watching the snow pile up on the branches, and sometimes she would land near Max's nest, just to check in and make sure everything was as it should be.

When the first signs of spring finally began to appear—the buds on the trees, the warmer breeze—Luna felt a surge of excitement. Soon, Max would wake up, and they would be reunited once again.

And sure enough, one bright morning, Max emerged from his nest, blinking in the sunlight and stretching his limbs after a long winter's sleep. As promised, Luna was there, waiting for him with a big smile on her face.

Lessons Learned

1. Change is a natural part of life, and it doesn't have to be scary.
2. True friendships can survive even long periods of separation.
3. Preparing for change makes it easier to adapt.
4. Small gestures, like a gift from a friend, can help us feel connected even when we're apart.
5. Time and distance don't diminish the bond of a strong friendship.
6. Seasonal changes are a reminder of life's cycles, and each

season brings its own opportunities.
7. Facing change with a positive mindset can make it easier to embrace new experiences.

Chapter 17: The Mysterious Owl

Max and Luna had always been curious about the old bell tower that stood at the edge of the city. It was a towering, ancient structure made of stone, its spire reaching high into the sky. The bell hadn't rung in years, and the tower was said to be abandoned, a relic of a time long past. But rumors had always swirled among the city's animals about a mysterious owl that lived in the bell tower, watching over the city from his lofty perch.

One evening, as the sun was setting and casting a golden glow over the city, Luna turned to Max with a gleam in her eye. "What do you think about visiting the old bell tower? I've heard the owl that lives there is full of wisdom and stories. Maybe he could teach us something."

Max hesitated. He had always been a little intimidated by the idea of meeting the owl. After all, the rumors painted him as an ancient, wise creature, and Max wasn't sure what to expect. But Luna's curiosity was infectious, and Max found himself nodding in agreement.

"All right," Max said. "Let's go see if we can meet this owl. But I have to admit, I'm a little nervous."

Luna laughed and gave Max a reassuring nudge. "Don't worry! I'm sure he's not as scary as the stories make him out to be."

Together, they made their way through the city, the sky growing darker as the evening turned into night. The streets were quiet, and the bell tower loomed ahead of them, its shadow stretching across the rooftops.

As they approached the tower, Max felt a chill run down his spine. The entrance was dark and foreboding, and the stone walls seemed to hum with an ancient energy. But Luna was undeterred. She flew up to the tower's entrance and peered inside.

"It's quiet," Luna whispered. "I think we can go in."

THE ADVENTURE OF TRUE FRIENDSHIP IN THE BIG CITY

Max took a deep breath and followed her inside, his paws echoing softly on the stone floor. The tower was dimly lit by the moonlight streaming in through the high windows, and the air was cool and still. They climbed a narrow spiral staircase that wound its way up to the top of the tower, each step creaking under their weight.

When they finally reached the top, they found themselves in a large, open room, the ceiling high above them. And there, perched on the edge of the bell, was the owl.

He was an imposing figure—his feathers were a deep shade of gray, almost blending into the shadows, and his eyes gleamed like amber in the dim light. He watched them with an air of quiet authority, his gaze steady and thoughtful.

"Who approaches my tower at this hour?" the owl asked, his voice deep and resonant, like the tolling of a distant bell.

Max froze, unsure of how to respond, but Luna stepped forward with her usual confidence. "My name is Luna, and this is my friend Max. We've heard about you—the wise owl of the bell tower. We wanted to meet you and see if you could share some of your wisdom with us."

The owl regarded them for a long moment, his eyes narrowing slightly as he studied them. Then, with a slow nod, he spread his wings and glided down to the floor, landing gracefully before them.

"I am called Orin," the owl said, his voice soft but commanding. "And wisdom, you say? Wisdom is not something I can simply give. It must be earned, learned through experience and reflection."

Max felt a little nervous under the owl's gaze, but Luna seemed unshaken. "We've had a lot of experiences," she said. "We've learned a lot about friendship, teamwork, and facing challenges. But we know there's always more to learn."

Orin tilted his head, considering her words. "Indeed. There is always more to learn. And it is wise of you to seek guidance."

Max found his voice and spoke up. "What kind of wisdom do you have to share with us? We're always looking to grow and become better friends, better adventurers."

Orin's eyes softened slightly, and he folded his wings neatly against his sides. "Friendship is a powerful force. It is one of the greatest gifts in life, and yet it is also one of the most challenging to maintain. Many seek friendships for the comfort and joy they bring, but few understand the true depth of what it means to be a friend."

Max and Luna exchanged a glance, curious about where Orin was going with this.

"The strength of a friendship," Orin continued, "lies not in the easy times, but in the difficult ones. True friends are those who stand by each other when the path is darkest, when the challenges seem insurmountable. It is in those moments that the bonds of friendship are tested and strengthened."

Max nodded slowly, thinking back to all the challenges he and Luna had faced together—the marathon, the storms, the adventures through the city. Each time, they had relied on each other to push through, and their friendship had grown stronger because of it.

"Challenges don't break friendships," Orin said, his amber eyes gleaming in the moonlight. "They reveal the strength within them."

Luna smiled, her eyes bright with understanding. "That makes sense. Every time Max and I face something tough, we come out of it even closer."

Orin gave a slow nod. "Exactly. It is easy to be a friend when times are good. But the true measure of friendship is found in how you support each other when things are difficult."

Max felt a surge of gratitude for Luna. She had always been there for him, pushing him to be brave, encouraging him when he felt unsure, and offering her unwavering support. Their friendship had been through its share of challenges, but those challenges had only made it stronger.

THE ADVENTURE OF TRUE FRIENDSHIP IN THE BIG CITY

Orin's deep voice broke through Max's thoughts. "As you continue your journey together, remember this: a true friend is not simply someone who shares in your joys. A true friend is one who stands with you in your sorrows, your fears, and your struggles. Nurture that bond, and it will carry you through the most difficult of times."

Max and Luna both nodded, the weight of Orin's words settling over them like a blanket. They had already learned so much about friendship, but Orin's wisdom had given them a new perspective—a deeper understanding of what it truly meant to be a friend.

"Thank you, Orin," Max said softly. "We'll remember your words."

Orin gave a slight bow of his head. "You are welcome. And remember, wisdom is not something you learn all at once. It comes with time, with reflection, and with experience. Continue to seek it, and you will find it in the most unexpected places."

With that, Orin spread his wings and flew back up to his perch on the bell, his silhouette dark against the night sky.

Max and Luna made their way back down the spiral staircase, their hearts full and their minds buzzing with new thoughts. As they stepped out into the cool night air, Max looked up at the tower, feeling a sense of awe for the wisdom Orin had shared with them.

Lessons Learned

1. Friendship is tested and strengthened during difficult times.
2. True friends stand by each other through challenges and hardships.
3. Wisdom is gained through experience and reflection, not all at once.
4. The strength of a friendship lies in how you support each other in tough times.
5. Friendship is a powerful bond that can carry you through life's challenges.
6. It's important to seek wisdom from those with experience

and knowledge.
7. Nurturing a friendship requires effort, understanding, and mutual support.

Chapter 18: The Night of the Lanterns

The Night of the Lanterns was a magical event that brought animals from all corners of the city together. It was a celebration of light, community, and the beauty of diversity. On this special night, animals from different neighborhoods gathered in the park, each bringing a brightly colored lantern to release into the sky. The lanterns symbolized hopes, dreams, and the connections that united the city's many different creatures.

Max and Luna had been looking forward to the Night of the Lanterns for weeks. Luna had told Max stories about how the sky would fill with colorful lights, each one representing the unique friendships and stories of the animals who lived in the city. It was a celebration of unity, where animals from all backgrounds came together to share their cultures, traditions, and experiences.

As the sun set on the evening of the event, Max and Luna made their way to the park, where a large crowd had already gathered. The air was filled with excitement and anticipation, and the trees were strung with twinkling lights that cast a warm glow over the scene. Animals of all kinds—birds, squirrels, rabbits, foxes, mice, and more—were milling about, holding their lanterns and chatting with one another.

"This is incredible," Max said, his eyes wide as he took in the scene. "I've never seen so many animals gathered in one place."

Luna smiled, her feathers ruffling with excitement. "That's the beauty of the Night of the Lanterns. It's not just about the lanterns—it's about coming together and celebrating our differences. Everyone brings their own traditions, and we all share in the experience."

Max looked around, noticing the variety of lanterns being carried by the different animals. Some were simple, made of paper and string, while others were elaborate creations, decorated with intricate patterns and symbols. Each lantern was unique, reflecting the individuality of the animals who had made them.

As they wandered through the crowd, Max and Luna met animals from all parts of the city. They listened to stories about different cultures, learning about the customs and traditions that made each group of animals special. Max was fascinated by the diversity he saw around him—each animal had their own way of celebrating, but they were all united by the same sense of community and friendship.

At one point, they met a family of hedgehogs who had traveled from a distant part of the city to participate in the event. The hedgehogs' lanterns were adorned with tiny stars, representing the constellation they believed guided their ancestors.

"Our family has been coming to the Night of the Lanterns for generations," one of the hedgehogs explained. "Each year, we add a new star to our lanterns to honor the friendships we've made and the lessons we've learned."

Max was deeply moved by the story. "That's beautiful," he said, looking at the lanterns with admiration. "It's amazing how different traditions can come together to create something so meaningful."

Luna nodded, her eyes bright with understanding. "That's what this night is all about. It's a celebration of our differences, but also of the things that bring us together."

As the time to release the lanterns drew closer, the excitement in the park grew. Animals gathered in small groups, preparing to let their lanterns take flight. Max and Luna found a quiet spot near the edge of the park, where they could watch the lanterns soar into the night sky.

Max held his lantern carefully, feeling the weight of the moment. Luna's lantern was a vibrant blue, decorated with swirling patterns that represented the adventures they had shared. Max's lantern was simpler, but it was filled with meaning—he had drawn small pictures of the moments that had defined his friendship with Luna, from their first meeting to their most recent adventures.

THE ADVENTURE OF TRUE FRIENDSHIP IN THE BIG CITY

"This is it," Luna said, her voice soft with anticipation. "Are you ready?"

Max nodded, his heart swelling with emotion. "I'm ready."

As the signal was given, animals all around the park began to release their lanterns. One by one, the lanterns floated into the sky, their glowing lights illuminating the darkness. Max and Luna watched in awe as the lanterns rose higher and higher, filling the night with color and light.

"It's beautiful," Max whispered, his eyes fixed on the sky. "I've never seen anything like it."

Luna smiled, her gaze also focused on the lanterns. "Each one of those lanterns represents a different friendship, a different story. But together, they create something even more beautiful."

Max felt a deep sense of connection to the animals around him. He realized that even though they all came from different places, with different backgrounds and experiences, they were all part of the same community. The Night of the Lanterns wasn't just a celebration of diversity—it was a celebration of unity.

As their lanterns joined the others in the sky, Max felt a sense of peace and gratitude. The night was a reminder that friendships, like the lanterns, could rise above any differences and light up the world in their own unique way.

After the lanterns had disappeared into the distance, the crowd began to gather around a large bonfire in the center of the park. Animals shared stories, songs, and food, each offering a glimpse into their own traditions. Max and Luna sat by the fire, listening to the voices around them and feeling a deep sense of belonging.

It was a cold, gray afternoon when Max and Luna first heard the soft whimpering coming from a narrow alley between two tall buildings. They had been walking through the city, enjoying the crisp autumn air, when the sound caught their attention. Max's ears perked up, and he stopped in his tracks, glancing at Luna with concern.

"Did you hear that?" Max asked, his voice barely above a whisper.

Luna nodded, her keen eyes scanning the alley. "It sounds like someone's in trouble. Let's check it out."

They cautiously approached the alley, the sound of the whimpering growing louder as they drew closer. As they rounded the corner, they found the source of the noise—a small, shivering puppy huddled against the wall, its fur matted and dirty. The puppy looked up at them with wide, frightened eyes, its little body trembling from the cold.

Max's heart immediately went out to the poor creature. "Oh no, it's just a puppy," he said softly, crouching down to get a better look. "It looks lost and scared."

Luna fluttered down beside Max, her eyes full of concern. "Where do you think it came from? It's so young—it must be lost."

The puppy whimpered again, its big eyes pleading for help. Max gently extended a paw, trying to comfort the little dog. "Hey there, it's okay. We're not going to hurt you."

The puppy hesitated for a moment but then slowly inched closer to Max, its tiny tail wagging ever so slightly. Max smiled, relieved that the puppy seemed to trust them.

"We can't just leave it here," Max said, his voice filled with determination. "We need to help it find its way home."

Luna nodded in agreement. "But how do we find out where it belongs? The city is so big—this little pup could have wandered from anywhere."

Max thought for a moment, his mind racing through possibilities. "Maybe we can ask around the neighborhood. Someone might have seen it before or know where it belongs."

With the puppy safely nestled between them, Max and Luna set off to ask the nearby animals if they had seen or heard anything about a missing puppy. They visited shopkeepers, chatted with other animals in the park, and even stopped by the local market to see if anyone recognized the little dog. But no one seemed to know where the puppy had come from.

Lessons Learned

1. Friendship transcends differences in culture, background, and experience.
2. Celebrating diversity can strengthen the bonds of community.
3. Every friendship is unique and brings its own light into the world.
4. Coming together with others helps us learn and grow.
5. Sharing traditions and stories can deepen understanding and connection.
6. The beauty of friendship lies in both its individuality and its unity.
7. True friendship lights up the world, just like the lanterns in the night sky.

Chapter 19: The Lost Puppy

As the day wore on, Max and Luna grew more concerned. The puppy was clearly tired, and the cold air wasn't helping its condition. Max could feel a sense of responsibility weighing heavily on him. This little dog needed their help, and he was determined to do everything he could to make sure it found its way home.

"We can't give up," Max said, his voice firm. "There has to be someone out there who's looking for this puppy."

Luna agreed, though her expression was filled with worry. "Maybe we should try putting up flyers. Someone might see them and recognize the puppy."

Max nodded. "That's a good idea. Let's head to the park and see if we can make some."

They quickly made their way to the park, where they gathered materials to create flyers. Luna, being the creative one, designed a simple but eye-catching flyer with a drawing of the puppy and a message that read, "Found: Lost Puppy. If you're missing a dog, please come to the park."

Once they had the flyers ready, Max and Luna set out to post them around the neighborhood. They tacked them up on trees, poles, and even near the entrances to the subway stations, hoping that someone would recognize the puppy and come forward.

As evening approached and the city grew quieter, Max and Luna returned to the park, feeling a little disheartened. They had done everything they could think of, but there was still no sign of the puppy's owner.

The puppy, now curled up in Max's lap, let out a soft sigh. Max gently stroked its fur, his heart heavy with worry. "What if no one comes for it?" Max asked quietly, looking up at Luna.

Luna's eyes softened as she perched beside him. "Then we'll find a way to take care of it ourselves. We won't let it stay lost."

THE ADVENTURE OF TRUE FRIENDSHIP IN THE BIG CITY

Max smiled at her words, feeling a renewed sense of hope. "You're right. We'll take care of it, no matter what."

Just as they were settling in for the evening, a voice called out from across the park. "Excuse me! Have you seen a little puppy?"

Max and Luna's heads snapped up, and they saw a young dog rushing toward them, her eyes filled with relief. The puppy in Max's lap immediately perked up, its tail wagging furiously.

"That's her!" the dog cried, her voice trembling with emotion. "That's my little sister! I've been looking for her everywhere!"

Max and Luna stood up, their hearts swelling with joy as the puppy bounded out of Max's lap and into the arms of its sister. The two dogs reunited with excited yips and tail wags, clearly overjoyed to be back together.

"Thank you so much," the older dog said, her eyes brimming with gratitude. "She wandered off earlier today, and I've been searching the whole city for her. I was so worried."

Max smiled, his heart filled with warmth. "We're just glad we could help. She's a sweet little pup."

Luna nodded in agreement. "We're happy she's found her way back to you."

As the dogs left the park, their tails wagging in unison, Max and Luna sat back down on the bench, their hearts full of satisfaction. They had taken responsibility for the puppy's safety, and in the end, their efforts had paid off.

"I'm glad we didn't give up," Max said, his voice filled with pride. "We did the right thing."

Luna smiled and gave him a gentle nudge. "You have a big heart, Max. That little puppy was lucky to have found you."

Max blushed at her words, but he couldn't deny the sense of fulfillment he felt. Helping the lost puppy had reminded him of the importance of compassion and responsibility. It wasn't always easy to take on the burdens of others, but it was always worth it in the end.

It started as an ordinary day in the city. Max and Luna were enjoying the cool breeze of the morning, walking through the park as they often did. The sun was still rising, casting a golden glow over the trees, and everything felt calm and peaceful. But as they continued their walk, something strange began to happen. The sky, which had been a clear blue just moments ago, started to change. A faint red hue spread across the horizon, growing darker and more intense with each passing minute.

Max stopped in his tracks, looking up at the sky with a mixture of confusion and concern. "Luna, look at the sky. What's happening?"

Luna, who had been darting ahead, paused and glanced upward. Her eyes widened as she took in the strange sight. "That's... not normal. The sky shouldn't be turning red like that."

As they watched, the red hue deepened, casting an eerie glow over the entire city. It was as if the sun had been replaced by something unnatural, and the once-clear air was now filled with a faint haze that made everything feel heavy.

"I've never seen anything like this before," Max said, his voice tinged with worry. "Do you think something's wrong?"

Luna fluttered down to perch beside him, her feathers ruffling with unease. "I don't know, but I don't like it. We should ask around and see if anyone knows what's going on."

They quickly made their way to the busy streets of the city, where animals were already starting to gather, all of them looking up at the sky with the same mixture of confusion and fear that Max and Luna felt. The red sky had become the topic of conversation, and it wasn't long before Max overheard a group of pigeons talking about the possibility of pollution.

"I heard the humans have been burning too much stuff," one pigeon said, flapping his wings in frustration. "That's why the air's so thick and the sky's gone red. It's all that pollution."

THE ADVENTURE OF TRUE FRIENDSHIP IN THE BIG CITY

Max felt a chill run down his spine. He had heard about pollution before, but he had never seen it affect the city like this. The idea that the air they were breathing could be harmful, that the sky could turn red from pollution, was frightening.

"We have to do something," Max said, turning to Luna with determination. "We can't just stand by while the city suffers. There has to be a way to help."

Luna nodded, her eyes reflecting the same urgency. "You're right. We can't fix everything ourselves, but maybe we can raise awareness. If everyone in the city understands how serious this is, we can work together to make a difference."

They quickly set to work, coming up with a plan to spread awareness about the dangers of pollution and the importance of keeping the city clean. Luna, with her natural talent for communication, flew from street to street, talking to groups of animals about the red sky and how pollution was likely to blame. Max, meanwhile, worked on creating posters with simple messages like, "Keep Our City Clean" and "Every Little Bit Helps."

Lessons Learned

1. Compassion is key when helping those in need.
2. Taking responsibility for others is an important part of being a good friend.
3. Never give up when trying to help someone—it's worth the effort.
4. Small acts of kindness can make a big difference in someone's life.
5. Working together to solve a problem strengthens relationships.
6. Helping others brings a sense of fulfillment and joy.
7. Empathy and care are essential qualities in building strong, supportive communities.

Chapter 20: The Day the Sky Turned Red

Over the next few days, the sky remained red, casting an unsettling shadow over the city. But thanks to Max and Luna's efforts, the animals began to take notice. Soon, small groups were forming to clean up the parks and streets, picking up litter and recycling whatever they could. The market vendors started using fewer plastic bags, and even the pigeons on the rooftops began organizing air patrols to monitor pollution levels from above.

Despite the ominous sky, there was a growing sense of hope in the city. Max and Luna saw that their efforts were making a real impact, and it filled them with a sense of pride. It wasn't just about cleaning up the city—it was about coming together as a community to protect their home.

One afternoon, as Max and Luna were resting in the park after a long day of organizing cleanup efforts, they noticed a shift in the air. The haze that had hung over the city for days seemed to be lifting, and the red tint in the sky was beginning to fade.

"Look, Max!" Luna exclaimed, pointing to the horizon. "The sky's clearing up!"

Max looked up, his heart swelling with relief. The sky, once a harsh red, was slowly returning to its natural blue. The city had made progress. It wasn't perfect, and there was still much work to be done, but the change in the sky felt like a sign that they were on the right track.

As the blue sky fully returned, animals throughout the city cheered, celebrating the progress they had made. Max and Luna smiled at each other, knowing that they had played a part in bringing the city together to fight for a cleaner, healthier environment.

"We did it," Max said, his voice filled with pride. "We made a difference."

THE ADVENTURE OF TRUE FRIENDSHIP IN THE BIG CITY

Luna nodded, her eyes bright with hope. "And we'll keep making a difference. This is just the beginning."

The city was buzzing with excitement as the annual Carnival of Lights approached. It was a time of joy and celebration, where every street and building was adorned with glowing lights that transformed the city into a magical wonderland. Animals from every neighborhood gathered to enjoy the festivities, and Max and Luna were no exception.

"This is my favorite event of the year," Luna said, her eyes sparkling with excitement as they made their way to the heart of the city. "There's just something so magical about seeing the city lit up like this."

Max had never experienced the Carnival of Lights before, and he couldn't wait to see what all the fuss was about. As they entered the city center, he was immediately struck by the sight before him. The streets were lined with strings of colorful lights, twinkling like stars against the evening sky. Lanterns hung from the trees, casting a warm glow over the bustling crowds below. It was as if the entire city had been transformed into a place of pure joy and wonder.

"This is incredible," Max said, his voice filled with awe. "I've never seen anything like it."

Luna grinned, her wings fluttering with excitement. "Just wait until we get to the main square. That's where the real magic happens."

They made their way through the crowds, stopping occasionally to admire the beautifully decorated stalls that lined the streets. Vendors were selling all kinds of treats candied fruits, warm pastries, and even sparkling drinks that seemed to glow in the dark. Max and Luna couldn't resist sampling a few of the delights as they wandered through the festival.

As they approached the main square, Max's breath caught in his throat. The sight before him was nothing short of breathtaking. A massive tree stood in the center of the square, its branches draped with thousands of tiny lights that shimmered like stars. Around the base of the tree, animals were gathered in a circle, singing and dancing, their faces glowing with happiness.

"This is what the Carnival of Lights is all about," Luna said, her voice soft with wonder. "It's a time to celebrate the beauty of life and the joy of being together with friends and family."

Max smiled, feeling a warmth spread through his chest. The atmosphere was infectious—everywhere he looked, animals were laughing, dancing, and enjoying the simple pleasures of the evening. It was a reminder that sometimes, the most important moments in life were the ones spent in celebration of the little things.

As the night wore on, Max and Luna joined in the dancing, spinning around the glowing tree with abandon. The music was lively, and the air was filled with the sound of laughter and joy. For a while, they forgot about everything else—the challenges they had faced, the worries of everyday life—and simply lived in the moment.

After the dancing, they found a quiet spot to sit and watch the fireworks display that was set to close out the evening. As the first bursts of color exploded in the sky, Max felt a deep sense of contentment. The Carnival of Lights wasn't just about the decorations or the festivities—it was about taking the time to appreciate the beauty of life and the friendships that made it all worthwhile.

Lessons Learned

1. It's important to take time to celebrate the joys of life.
2. Small moments of happiness can make a big difference in our overall well-being.
3. Sharing joyful experiences with friends strengthens the bond of friendship.
4. Celebration helps us appreciate the beauty of everyday moments.
5. Laughter, music, and dancing are simple pleasures that bring people together.

6. The magic of life is often found in the little things we take time to enjoy.
7. Taking time for joy and relaxation is essential to balance life's challenges.

Chapter 21: The Heart of the City

One morning, as the city bustled with its usual activity, Luna suggested they take a trip to the heart of the city—a place where the oldest and most historic landmarks stood. Max had heard stories about this part of the city, but he had never ventured there himself. Luna, ever the adventurer, insisted that it was a journey worth making.

"There's something special about seeing the history of the city," Luna said as they walked along the cobblestone streets. "It reminds you of all the lives that have been lived here and all the stories that have been told."

Max nodded, intrigued by the idea. As they ventured deeper into the city, the buildings became older, their walls worn with age and their windows framed by ivy. The streets grew narrower, and the noise of the bustling market faded into the background, replaced by the soft hum of history.

Their first stop was an old clock tower, its face cracked but still ticking away the hours. Luna fluttered up to the top, perching on one of the hands as she gazed out over the city.

"Imagine how many animals have watched the city grow from this very spot," Luna said, her voice full of wonder. "This tower has stood here for hundreds of years, keeping time while the city changed around it."

Max smiled, appreciating the weight of her words. The city had indeed changed over the years, but the clock tower remained a steadfast reminder of the passage of time and the history that had shaped their world.

Next, they visited a grand statue in the center of a small square. The statue depicted a pair of animals—one bird and one squirrel—standing side by side, their heads held high. A plaque at the base of the statue read, "In honor of friendship, unity, and the strength of community."

THE ADVENTURE OF TRUE FRIENDSHIP IN THE BIG CITY

Max felt a lump form in his throat as he looked at the statue. It reminded him of his own friendship with Luna, and all the challenges they had faced together.

"This could be us one day," Luna said with a grin. "Maybe someone will build a statue of us and our adventures."

Max chuckled, though the thought warmed his heart. "I don't know about that, but it's a nice idea."

As they continued their journey through the heart of the city, Max found himself reflecting on everything they had been through. From their first meeting on Main Street to the countless adventures that had followed, Max and Luna had grown closer with each passing day. Their friendship had been tested by challenges, strengthened by teamwork, and deepened by the many lessons they had learned along the way.

As they walked through the quiet streets, Max turned to Luna, his voice soft with gratitude. "I'm glad we've had all these adventures together. I don't know what I'd do without you."

Luna smiled, her eyes filled with affection. "I feel the same way, Max. We've been through a lot, but it's made us stronger. And no matter what happens, I know we'll always be there for each other."

Max nodded, feeling a deep sense of peace settle over him. Their friendship had grown from something small and unexpected into something powerful and enduring. It wasn't just about the adventures—they had learned to support each other, to listen, to laugh, and to face whatever life threw their way.

As they reached the final stop on their tour—a beautiful old fountain in the center of a quiet square—Max and Luna sat down on the edge of the fountain, watching the water sparkle in the sunlight.

"This place is like the heart of the city," Luna said, her voice soft. "It's where everything began, and it's where the spirit of the city lives."

Max nodded, his heart full. "It's like our friendship. It's grown and changed, but at the core, it's still the same."

They sat in comfortable silence for a while, simply enjoying the peace and beauty of the moment. It was a time of reflection, a chance to look back on all they had been through and to appreciate how far they had come.

Lessons Learned

1. Reflection helps us appreciate how far we've come in life.
2. True friendships grow and deepen over time.
3. Every journey is shaped by the experiences and challenges we face.
4. The heart of a friendship is built on trust, support, and shared memories.
5. History reminds us of the importance of community and unity.
6. Taking time to appreciate the past helps us prepare for the future.
7. Strong friendships, like cities, are built over time and can withstand the test of time.

Chapter 22: The Goodbye That Wasn't

Max had always known that someday, he might have to leave the city, even if only for a little while. But when the news came that his family needed him to visit the countryside for an extended stay, the reality of saying goodbye to Luna hit him harder than he had expected.

Max had spent the entire morning pacing in his nest, his mind racing with thoughts of what it would be like to leave Luna behind. They had shared so many adventures, and the idea of being apart for weeks, or even months, filled him with a deep sense of sadness.

He knew he had to tell her, but he wasn't sure how. Max and Luna had faced plenty of challenges together, but this felt different. It wasn't something they could solve or work through—it was simply a part of life.

That afternoon, Max finally gathered the courage to meet Luna in the park. As usual, she was flying between the trees, her wings catching the sunlight as she darted through the branches. When she saw Max approaching, she landed beside him with a bright smile.

"Hey, Max! What's going on?" she asked, her usual energy filling the air.

Max took a deep breath, his paws fidgeting nervously. "Luna... I have something to tell you."

Luna's smile faltered slightly, her eyes searching his face. "What is it?"

"I have to leave the city for a while," Max said, his voice heavy with emotion. "My family needs me to go to the countryside. I don't know how long I'll be gone."

Luna's eyes widened in surprise, and for a moment, she didn't say anything. Max could see the shock and sadness on her face, and it made his heart ache.

"Leave?" Luna asked softly, her voice filled with disbelief. "But... what about everything we've been doing? What about all the adventures we've planned?"

Max looked down at his paws, struggling to find the right words. "I don't want to go, Luna. But I have to. My family needs me, and I can't let them down."

Luna's feathers ruffled with unease, and she took a deep breath, trying to process the news. "I understand, Max. Family is important. But... I'm going to miss you. I'm going to miss you a lot."

Max's heart sank at the sight of Luna's sadness. He had known this goodbye would be hard, but seeing how much it affected her made it even more difficult.

"I'll miss you too," Max said, his voice thick with emotion. "But this doesn't have to be the end. We'll stay in touch, and when I come back, we'll pick up right where we left off."

Luna nodded, though her eyes were filled with unshed tears. "You promise?"

Max smiled, though it was a little sad. "I promise. This isn't goodbye forever. It's just... see you later."

Luna managed a small smile, though Max could see the weight of the goodbye in her eyes. "Okay. I'll hold you to that."

For the next few days, Max and Luna spent every moment they could together, enjoying their favorite spots in the park and talking about all the adventures they would have when Max returned. But the day of his departure finally arrived, and Max found himself standing at the edge of the park, his bags packed and ready to go.

Luna stood beside him, her usual energy replaced by a quiet sadness. "I guess this is it," she said softly.

Max nodded, his heart heavy. "I'll be back before you know it."

Luna smiled, though it didn't quite reach her eyes. "I'll be here waiting."

THE ADVENTURE OF TRUE FRIENDSHIP IN THE BIG CITY

With one last hug, Max turned and began his journey to the countryside, leaving behind the city he had come to love and the friend who had become like family. As he walked, he couldn't help but feel a sense of loss, knowing that he wouldn't see Luna's bright smile or hear her laughter for a while.

But as the days passed, Max realized that their friendship was stronger than any distance. He and Luna wrote letters to each other, sharing stories about their daily lives and reminiscing about their adventures. And even though they were miles apart, Max felt as if Luna was still right there beside him, cheering him on and offering her support.

Weeks turned into months, and though Max enjoyed his time in the countryside, he couldn't wait to return to the city. He missed the hustle and bustle of city life, the familiar streets and parks, but most of all, he missed Luna.

One bright morning, after what felt like an eternity, Max finally made his way back to the city. As he approached the park, his heart raced with excitement. He couldn't wait to see Luna again, to tell her all about his adventures in the countryside and to hear what she had been up to in his absence.

When Max reached their favorite spot in the park, he was greeted by the sight of Luna, perched on a branch, her eyes scanning the horizon. As soon as she saw him, her face lit up with pure joy, and she flew down to greet him, her wings fluttering with excitement.

"Max!" she cried, her voice filled with happiness. "You're back!"

Max chuckled, feeling a sense of peace wash over him. "And I can't wait to hear what you've been up to. I'm sure you've had plenty of adventures without me."

Luna's eyes twinkled mischievously. "Oh, you know it. But nothing compares to the adventures we'll have now that you're back."

Lessons Learned

1. True friendships can withstand time and distance.
2. Goodbyes are often temporary in strong friendships.
3. Staying connected, even from afar, helps keep friendships alive.
4. The strength of a friendship is not measured by proximity, but by the bond shared.
5. Separation can make friendships stronger by deepening appreciation.
6. Even when apart, friends remain an important part of each other's lives.
7. Reunions are sweeter when you know the bond of friendship is unbreakable

Chapter 23: The Grand Reunion

Max had only been back in the city for a few days when Luna announced her plan for a grand celebration. "We need to throw a party to celebrate your return!" she declared, her eyes gleaming with excitement.

Max laughed, though he couldn't help but feel a little flustered. "A party? For me? That's not necessary, Luna. I'm just happy to be back."

But Luna was having none of it. "Nonsense! We've been apart for too long, and now that you're back, we need to celebrate properly. We've had so many adventures together, and this is the perfect way to remind ourselves of everything we've accomplished."

Max couldn't argue with that. In truth, he was thrilled to be back, and the idea of a celebration sounded like the perfect way to reunite with all the friends they had made throughout their adventures. So, with Luna taking the lead, they set to work planning the grand reunion.

For the next few days, Luna was a whirlwind of activity. She flew from one end of the city to the other, inviting everyone they knew to the party. Max, meanwhile, helped set up decorations in the park and prepare the food. He had never been one for big parties, but Luna's enthusiasm was infectious, and soon he found himself looking forward to the event.

When the day of the grand reunion finally arrived, the park was transformed into a festive wonderland. Colorful banners hung from the trees, and lanterns were strung along the pathways, casting a warm glow over the scene. Tables were laden with food and drinks, and a small stage had been set up for music and dancing.

As the guests began to arrive, Max felt a rush of happiness. There were familiar faces everywhere—animals from all parts of the city, each one representing a different adventure or lesson Max and Luna had learned along the way. There were the squirrels and pigeons from the subway adventure, the friends they had made during the City

Marathon, and even the mischievous monkey they had helped in the park.

Luna, as always, was at the center of it all, greeting everyone with her usual warmth and energy. "This is going to be the best celebration ever!" she said, her eyes sparkling as she fluttered down to Max's side.

Max smiled, feeling a deep sense of contentment. "It already is," he said softly. "I can't believe how many friends we've made over the past year. It's amazing to see everyone here."

Luna nodded, her expression turning thoughtful. "We've been through so much together, Max. And I think this party is the perfect way to celebrate not just your return, but everything we've accomplished. We've learned so many lessons, faced so many challenges, and grown stronger because of it."

As the evening wore on, the celebration reached its peak. Music filled the air, and animals danced and laughed, enjoying the festive atmosphere. Max and Luna spent the night catching up with old friends, sharing stories about their adventures and reflecting on all the lessons they had learned.

At one point, as the sun began to set and the lanterns glowed brighter, Luna called for everyone's attention. She fluttered up to the stage, her voice carrying over the crowd. "I just want to say a few words to thank everyone for coming," she began, her eyes shining with emotion. "This celebration is more than just a reunion—it's a reminder of the power of friendship and the incredible journey we've all been on together."

She turned to Max, her smile warm and full of affection. "Max, you've been my partner through so many adventures, and I'm so grateful to have you as my friend. We've learned that true friendship is about more than just having fun together—it's about supporting each other through challenges, growing together, and never giving up on each other."

THE ADVENTURE OF TRUE FRIENDSHIP IN THE BIG CITY

Max felt a lump form in his throat as the crowd cheered, their faces glowing with admiration for Luna's words.

"We've faced storms, races, mysteries, and even separations," Luna continued, her voice strong. "But through it all, our friendship has only grown stronger. And that's something worth celebrating."

The crowd erupted into applause, and Max couldn't help but feel a surge of pride. Luna had captured exactly what he had been feeling—their journey together had been about more than just the adventures. It had been about the bond they had formed and the lessons they had learned along the way.

As the applause died down, Luna fluttered back to Max's side, her eyes twinkling with mischief. "Now let's get back to the party!"

It was a bright, breezy afternoon when Luna swooped down to Max's nest, her wings fluttering with excitement. She landed lightly on a branch, her eyes gleaming with mischief.

"Max! You'll never guess what I found out!" she exclaimed, unable to contain her excitement.

Max looked up from his pile of acorns, intrigued by her energy. "What is it, Luna? You look like you're ready to burst!"

Luna fluffed her feathers proudly. "I overheard some of the pigeons talking. They say there's a hidden treasure somewhere in the park! Apparently, it's been there for ages, buried by animals who wanted to keep it safe."

Max's ears perked up. A hidden treasure? That sounded like an adventure he couldn't pass up.

"A treasure? Are you sure it's not just a rumor?" Max asked, though his curiosity was already piqued.

Luna shrugged playfully. "Even if it is, wouldn't it be fun to try and find it? I think it's worth a shot!"

Max chuckled, knowing that Luna had already made up her mind. "All right, count me in. But where do we even start looking?"

Luna pulled out a small, crumpled map from under her wing. "I got this from one of the older pigeons. It's a rough sketch of the park, with some clues on where the treasure might be hidden. We just have to follow the hints."

Max stared at the map, which was filled with squiggly lines and cryptic notes. It didn't look like much to him, but Luna was already studying it with great enthusiasm.

"The first clue says, 'Where the tallest tree touches the sky, look beneath where roots lie,'" Luna read aloud, her brow furrowed in concentration.

Max thought for a moment. "The tallest tree in the park... That's got to be the old oak by the lake! Its roots stretch out in every direction."

Luna nodded, clearly impressed. "Exactly! Let's start there."

The two friends set off toward the old oak tree, their excitement growing with each step. The park was peaceful, with birds chirping and the occasional squirrel darting across the path. As they neared the oak, Max felt a familiar sense of adventure bubbling up inside him.

When they reached the tree, Luna flew up to perch on one of the low branches, while Max examined the ground near the roots.

"Do you see anything?" Luna called down, her feathers rustling in the breeze.

Max crouched down, brushing away some leaves and dirt. At first, there was nothing unusual, just the gnarly roots of the old oak. But then, his paw hit something solid. He brushed away more dirt and uncovered a small, weathered stone with strange markings on it.

"Luna, come look at this!" Max exclaimed, his heart pounding with excitement.

Luna flew down and landed beside him, her eyes wide as she studied the stone. "That has to be part of the treasure! What do the markings mean?"

THE ADVENTURE OF TRUE FRIENDSHIP IN THE BIG CITY

Max squinted at the symbols, trying to make sense of them. "I think it's another clue. Look, there's a picture of what looks like... water? Maybe it's pointing us to the lake."

Luna nodded eagerly. "Let's go! We're getting closer!"

They rushed toward the lake, their minds racing with thoughts of what the treasure could be. As they reached the water's edge, they scanned the area for any signs of the next clue. Max spotted a small pile of stones near the shore and hurried over to investigate.

"Here! There's something carved into these stones," Max said, pointing to the faint markings.

Luna landed beside him, her eyes gleaming. "Another clue!"

The stones had an image of a small bridge, along with an arrow pointing toward the north side of the park.

"That's the footbridge near the old garden," Luna said excitedly. "Come on!"

They followed the trail, their anticipation building with each step. The footbridge was a peaceful spot, usually quiet and overlooked by most animals. As they reached the bridge, Max and Luna paused, scanning the area for any sign of the treasure.

"Look over there," Max said, pointing to a small, hidden alcove under the bridge. "It's perfect for hiding something."

Luna fluttered over to the alcove, and sure enough, there was a small wooden box, half-buried in the dirt. Her heart raced as she pulled it out and placed it gently on the ground.

"We found it!" Luna exclaimed, her voice full of excitement. "The treasure!"

Lessons Learned

1. True friendship is worth celebrating.
2. Reflecting on shared experiences strengthens the bond between friends.
3. Friendship is about more than just having fun—it's about

support, growth, and resilience.
4. The journey of friendship is ongoing, with new adventures always on the horizon.
5. Celebrations are an important way to mark milestones and honor the people we care about.
6. Reunions remind us of the enduring power of friendship, no matter the challenges faced.
7. The best adventures in life are the ones we share with the friends who stand by us through everything.

Chapter 24: The Whispering Wind

Max could hardly believe it. The box was old and weathered, its surface worn smooth from years of being hidden away. With a sense of awe, he opened the lid, revealing a collection of small, sparkling trinkets—tiny gemstones, old coins, and a beautifully crafted locket.

"It's beautiful," Max said softly, his eyes wide with wonder. "I can't believe we actually found it."

Luna smiled, her heart swelling with pride. "It wasn't just about the treasure, Max. It was about the adventure, and the fun we had along the way."

Max nodded, realizing she was right. The real treasure had been the excitement of the hunt, the thrill of solving each clue, and the joy of sharing the experience with his best friend.

As they sat together, admiring the little box of trinkets, Max felt a deep sense of gratitude for the adventures they shared. The treasure was a reminder that life was full of surprises, and sometimes, the greatest rewards weren't material at all—they were the memories and friendships forged along the way.

"Thanks, Luna," Max said with a smile. "I wouldn't have found this without you."

Luna grinned, her eyes twinkling. "I wouldn't have wanted to do it without you, Max. Here's to more adventures, and to whatever treasures we find next!"

It was a quiet, peaceful day in the city, and the gentle breeze that blew through the trees made everything feel calm and serene. Max and Luna had decided to spend the afternoon in their favorite part of the park, enjoying the fresh air and the sounds of nature. The day felt perfect—until the wind began to change.

At first, it was just a slight shift in the breeze, a cool gust that rustled the leaves a little more forcefully than before. But soon, the wind began to grow stronger, swirling around them in strange patterns. Max's fur ruffled as he looked up at Luna with a puzzled expression.

"Is it just me, or does the wind seem... different today?" Max asked, his voice tinged with curiosity.

Luna, who was perched on a branch above him, tilted her head as she felt the breeze ruffle her feathers. "You're right, Max. It's not just a normal wind—it feels like it's trying to tell us something."

Max raised an eyebrow. "The wind? Telling us something?"

Luna nodded, her eyes wide with intrigue. "Haven't you ever heard of the Whispering Wind? Some animals say that when the wind blows in a certain way, it carries messages—if you listen closely, you can hear them."

Max was skeptical, but Luna's excitement was contagious. "All right," he said with a smile. "I'm willing to listen. What do you think the wind is saying?"

Luna closed her eyes, letting the breeze flow through her feathers as she concentrated. The wind picked up slightly, whistling through the trees with a faint, melodic sound. Luna's eyes flew open, and she gasped.

"Max, I think it's telling us to follow it!"

Max blinked in surprise. "Follow the wind? How do we even do that?"

Luna grinned, her wings fluttering with excitement. "Just trust me! The wind is blowing in a certain direction, and I think it's leading us somewhere. Come on!"

With that, Luna took off, flying in the direction of the breeze. Max, still unsure but intrigued by the idea, followed close behind, weaving through the trees as the wind guided them along the path. The further they went, the stronger the wind seemed to blow, swirling around them as if it were urging them onward.

"This way!" Luna called, her voice barely audible over the gusts. "I think we're getting closer!"

THE ADVENTURE OF TRUE FRIENDSHIP IN THE BIG CITY

Max wasn't sure where they were going, but he trusted Luna's instincts. They followed the wind as it led them deeper into the park, past familiar landmarks and into areas they rarely explored. The trees grew taller, and the sounds of the city faded into the background until all that remained was the rustling of the leaves and the whisper of the wind.

Finally, they reached a small clearing, tucked away in a quiet corner of the park. The wind suddenly died down, leaving the air still and silent. Max and Luna exchanged glances, their hearts pounding with anticipation.

Max hurried over to where Luna was pointing. Sure enough, there was an old carving on the tree, worn by time but still visible. It wasn't just any carving—it was a series of symbols, much like the ones they had seen during their treasure hunt. This time, however, the symbols seemed to form a pattern, almost like a map.

"This must be a message," Luna said, her voice full of excitement. "The Whispering Wind led us here for a reason."

Max studied the symbols, feeling the thrill of discovery. "It looks like some sort of puzzle. Maybe if we figure it out, we'll understand why the wind brought us here."

Luna fluttered to his side, inspecting the symbols closely. "I think you're right. The pattern starts at the bottom and moves upward, like a path."

Max ran his paw over the carvings, tracing the symbols carefully. "Maybe the wind was leading us to something that's been hidden here for a long time. Something we're meant to find."

Lessons Learned

1. Sometimes, nature has its own way of guiding us.
2. Curiosity leads to incredible discoveries when we're willing to follow the unknown.
3. Trusting your instincts can reveal hidden treasures.

4. The magic of the world is often found in unexpected places.
5. Listening closely to your surroundings can open the door to new adventures.
6. Patience and teamwork are key to solving mysteries together.
7. The greatest treasures are often reminders of the beauty and wonder around us.

Chapter 25: The Festival of Friends

Together, Max and Luna began piecing together the meaning of the symbols. As they worked, the breeze returned, swirling gently around them as if encouraging their progress. The symbols seemed to point toward a particular spot in the clearing, not far from the tree where the carving was etched.

"There," Luna said, her voice filled with anticipation. "I think it's leading us to that patch of ground."

Max followed her gaze and walked over to the spot she had indicated. The ground looked unremarkable at first, but as he brushed away some leaves, he noticed something buried just beneath the surface—a small wooden box, much like the one they had found during the treasure hunt.

"Another box!" Max exclaimed, his heart racing. "Do you think this is the treasure?"

Luna landed beside him, her eyes shining. "Only one way to find out!"

With gentle paws, Max carefully lifted the box from the earth. It was old and worn, but the lock was intact. Luna, ever resourceful, found a small stone and tapped it against the lock until it gave way with a soft click.

Max opened the box, and inside was something that took his breath away—a delicate, glowing feather, unlike anything he had ever seen. The feather shimmered with an ethereal light, casting a soft glow over the clearing.

"What... what is this?" Max whispered, his voice filled with awe.

Luna's eyes were wide with wonder. "I've never seen anything like it. It looks magical."

Max gently lifted the feather from the box, holding it up to the light. As he did, the wind began to swirl around them again, more intense this time, but not chaotic. It was as if the wind was celebrating the discovery, dancing with the feather's glow.

"The Whispering Wind brought us here for this," Luna said, her voice soft with realization. "It wanted us to find this feather."

Max smiled, feeling a deep sense of connection to the wind, the feather, and the adventure they had just experienced. "It's beautiful. But what does it mean?"

Luna thought for a moment, then her face brightened. "I think it's a reminder—of the power of nature, of the mysteries all around us, and of the adventures we can find if we listen closely and follow where the wind takes us."

Max nodded, feeling a sense of peace settle over him. "You're right, Luna. This feather is more than just a treasure. It's a symbol of everything we've learned—about curiosity, trust, and the magic of the world around us."

As they sat in the clearing, the wind continued to swirl gently, as if thanking them for listening. Max held the glowing feather close, knowing that this adventure, like so many others, had brought them closer not just to each other, but to the world they lived in.

The city was buzzing with excitement as the annual Festival of Friends approached. It was a special time when animals from all corners of the city gathered to celebrate friendship, unity, and the bonds that made their lives richer. Everywhere Max and Luna went, they could see preparations underway—banners being hung, food stalls being set up, and animals chatting excitedly about the festivities to come.

"This year's festival is going to be the biggest one yet!" Luna said, her eyes gleaming with anticipation as they made their way through the bustling streets. "There's going to be music, games, performances, and the grand Friendship Parade at the end!"

Max smiled, feeling the same sense of excitement that had spread through the city. "I've been looking forward to this for weeks. It's a chance to celebrate everything we've been through with all our friends."

As they walked, they passed groups of animals decorating the streets with colorful flowers, while others worked on constructing floats for the parade. The air was filled with the sound of laughter and joy, and Max couldn't help but feel grateful for the sense of community that surrounded him.

"Let's go find a good spot for the parade later," Max suggested, eager to make the most of the day.

Luna nodded, and they made their way to the central square, where the festival's main events would take place. The square was already bustling with activity—animals were setting up stalls selling all kinds of delicious treats, while others prepared for the games and contests that would happen throughout the day.

Max and Luna decided to start with one of their favorite games: the three-legged race. The race required teamwork and coordination, and it had become a festival tradition for them to compete together each year.

"Ready, Max?" Luna asked with a grin as they lined up with the other teams.

Max chuckled, already feeling the excitement building. "Always! Let's win this!"

As the race began, Max and Luna worked together, their movements perfectly synchronized as they dashed down the path, tied at the leg. They laughed as they stumbled and regained their balance, keeping pace with the other teams. By the time they reached the finish line, they were out of breath but smiling from ear to ear.

"We didn't win," Max said, still catching his breath, "but that was so much fun!"

Luna grinned, her feathers ruffling with joy. "It's not about winning—it's about having fun with your best friend."

The rest of the day was filled with similar moments of joy. Max and Luna visited various stalls, played games, and tasted all kinds of treats. They met up with old friends they had made during their many adventures, each one sharing stories and laughter as they celebrated the bonds that had brought them together.

As the sun began to set, casting a golden glow over the square, the highlight of the festival arrived—the Friendship Parade. Max and Luna found a spot near the front of the crowd, eager to watch the floats pass by. Each float was decorated with bright, colorful designs, showcasing the creativity and uniqueness of the different neighborhoods in the city.

As the parade rolled by, Max couldn't help but feel a sense of awe. It wasn't just the beautiful floats or the cheerful music that filled the air—it was the sense of unity that brought everyone together. Animals of all kinds, from every part of the city, were celebrating the same thing: the power of friendship.

When the final float passed, a grand display of fireworks lit up the night sky, casting shimmering colors across the city. Max and Luna watched in silence, their hearts full as they reflected on the meaning of the festival.

"This festival reminds me of everything we've been through," Max said softly, his eyes still fixed on the sky. "All the adventures, the challenges, the fun. We've learned so much, and it's all because of our friendship."

Luna smiled, her eyes shining with affection. "You're right, Max. We've been through so much together, and this festival is a celebration of that. It's a reminder that no matter where life takes us, our friendship will always be the most important thing."

Max nodded, feeling a deep sense of gratitude. "I wouldn't trade it for anything."

As the final fireworks burst overhead, Max and Luna stood side by side, knowing that their friendship was stronger than ever. The Festival of Friends had been a celebration of more than just a day of fun—it had been a reminder of the bond they had built, the adventures they had shared, and the countless memories they had yet to make.

THE ADVENTURE OF TRUE FRIENDSHIP IN THE BIG CITY

Lessons Learned

1. The journey is often more important than the destination.
2. Teamwork and communication make challenges more fun and rewarding.
3. Solving problems together strengthens friendships.
4. Adventure can be found in unexpected places.
5. The true treasures in life are the memories and experiences shared with friends.
6. Curiosity and persistence lead to exciting discoveries.
7. Enjoying the process makes the reward even sweeter.

Don't miss out!

Visit the website below and you can sign up to receive emails whenever Eleanor Sutton publishes a new book. There's no charge and no obligation.

https://books2read.com/r/B-A-MAILC-QTEBF

BOOKS 2 READ

Connecting independent readers to independent writers.

Did you love *The Adventure of True Friendship in the Big City*? Then you should read *Respecting Others Brings Us Closer*[1] by Skye Forrest!

Respecting Others Brings Us Closer is a heartwarming collection of 20 enchanting stories set in the diverse, magical villages of a fantastical world. Each tale explores the power of respect, kindness, and understanding in building meaningful connections and fostering community.

From a timid dragon finding friendship, to a hidden garden that blossoms under care, to a mysterious lake that reflects the emotions of its people, these stories reveal how respect can transform lives, heal wounds, and bring us closer together.

---

1. https://books2read.com/u/47BEWq

2. https://books2read.com/u/47BEWq

Perfect for young readers, this book teaches timeless lessons about empathy, patience, and the value of seeing the world through the eyes of others.

Also by Eleanor Sutton

Community and Society
The Adventure of True Friendship in the Big City

Virtue Series
How the Kindness Seed Grew Into a Giant Tree

About the Author

Eleanor Sutton crafts emotionally rich children's books that dive into the complexities of growing up with grace, courage, and empathy. Her stories are filled with vivid moments where characters face real-life challenges, learning the values of honesty, kindness, and bravery along the way. Eleanor's unique ability to balance heartwarming narratives with meaningful lessons helps children not only understand their own feelings but also appreciate the beauty of inclusivity and the strength found in unity.

The Good Child

Inspiring values and fellowship

About the Publisher

The Good Child Academy is a premier publisher dedicated to creating enchanting and educational children's books that inspire imagination and creativity. With a focus on delivering high-quality stories, the academy collaborates with talented authors and illustrators to produce books that captivate young minds. Specializing in themes like adventure, learning, and seasonal celebrations such as Halloween, Good Child Academy ensures that each book fosters curiosity, empathy, and a love for reading. Their mission is to nurture the next generation of lifelong readers.

Read more at https://www.patreon.com/thegoodchild/shop.

Milton Keynes UK
Ingram Content Group UK Ltd.
UKHW032315121024
449481UK00011B/363